Skeleτon s Hand

by Robert English

Dedication

This book is dedicated to Geoff and Wally, two friends who left this world too early.

Prologue

For everything, there is a season, and a time for every matter under heaven.

Ecclesiastes 3: 1

By the late 1960's, the drug business was booming in Canada thanks largely to innovative smugglers that craved the feel and taste of money. From South America, through the USA, to the streets of every city in Canada, the problem was reaching epidemic levels. Response by police was limited as governments argued over who was going to pay extra for resources to tackle the plague of cocaine and heroin.

In those early years, policing was relegated to a small number of select agencies including the FBI, the RCMP, both country's Customs agencies and local police forces. As Canada Customs struggled to stop drugs coming into Canada, the smugglers found more unique ways of hiding their precious cargo. It was almost like a game with the agents discovering everything from hollowed out canes, to bags tucked inside bicycle tires, to saltshakers in campers, all filled with drugs. In most cases, these were users with their own supply and having the bad luck to be caught. The transport truck traffic was much harder to monitor as they carried sealed containers crossing the border every minute of every day, containers that offered hundreds of hiding places.

The most difficult seizures of large quantities took planning, especially when Canada and US Customs worked jointly to stop highly organized smuggling operations. Success was often reliant on tips and it was a real bonus if the agents could seize both the smuggler and the buyer.

In 1976, Canadian authorities were alerted that a truck would be transporting over sixty pounds of cocaine, a larger than usual load. The trucker would stop in Billings Montana and pick up bags of the drug, making sure they were well hidden in his cargo. He would then cross from Montana to Alberta at Coutts. Once across the border, and fifty miles into Alberta, he would offload twelve five-pound bags of uncut drugs to four specialty riders of a motorcycle gang.

The riders would transport the bags to an exchange location between the pickup point and Calgary and hand the cocaine over to two men who would pay the riders. Once the exchange was complete, the two groups would disperse.

After a month of planning, the second week of October was set for an ambush by authorities. The plan was simple. Team 1 would arrest the trucker's US supplier as soon as the truck crossed the border. Team 2 would arrest the trucker after he dropped off the drugs and the bikers were long gone. Team 3, the largest team, would set up an ambush at the location where the bikers were to exchange the drugs for money. It all sounded so simple.

Team 3 was well hidden near an abandoned gas station where they were told the exchange was to take place at five fifteen in the afternoon. The bikers arrived shortly after five and a black sedan pulled up at exactly five fifteen. As soon as two men exited the car, the authorities moved in and bullets flew. During the melee, two of the Canadian officers were shot, one in the leg and the other in the shoulder. One of the bikers and both men from the car were killed. The three remaining bikers were taken into custody.

The Captain in charge was very specific with the tactical team. Once the takedown was completed, every piece of evidence must remain in place until the photographer took pictures. Each team member was to prepare an independent report and deposit it on the Captain's desk by noon the next day. He knew that both the American and Canadian justice system needed as much primary evidence as possible to ensure convictions. Finally, the cleanup crew would come in, collect, bag, and label everything. The weapons, drugs and cash were to be secured in zippered canvas bags and locked.

What the reports failed to include was a secret, a skeleton buried deep in the closet, and that skeleton had a hand in a longer story

Chapter 1

The cool autumn ride through the light Calgary traffic was unusually uncomfortable on his 1974 Harley Davison Softail. It was a big cruising bike but still prone to send vibrations up the arms when it hit potholes and rough pavement, especially when he felt cold. The only good thing about the ride was the 'respect' that the public and the police gave him when they saw the patch on the back of his black leather jacket – Dark Destiny MC.

It was a trip that Joey Parsons would not normally make alone but the big Club's Sergeant at Arms had summoned him. The ride from his house on the west side, to the clubhouse on the east side, was less than an hour but each minute told Joey Parsons' gut that it couldn't be personal; they didn't summon men to meetings with the Club President if it was for a serious violation. For those indiscretions against the code of the Club, a small crew was dispatched to deal with the issue, always with a tragic result. No, this had to be about the operation that his small group of bikers called the Skeletons Hand was involved in, a team of four who were together for the past three years. Looking back it had been four years since he received full patch privileges and he worked hard to get to the point of being responsible for the special group of Dark Destiny.

As he drove up to the gated clubhouse on a remote street with very few other houses, there was the usual collection of pristine motorcycles lined up in a perfect row. Three 'prospects' stood outside the main door smoking. As soon as they saw his Dark Destiny Motorcycle Club

5

patch, all three moved quickly toward him, the first ready to take his bike and park it. He dismounted leaving his black leather gloves on the seat. One prospect already held a rag in his hand ready to shine the chrome. Parsons remembered those early days and generated a quick smile.

A dozen pair of hardened steely eyes turned to him as he walked through the reinforced door of the house. Acrid smoke filled the room and the tension returned to laughter and conversation as they recognized his patch. Members of the gang learned long ago that all gangs respected the 'Dark Destiny' patch. Parsons nodded to them as they tipped their glasses when he walked by. Brian Hills, the Sergeant at Arms, was the first to come over and shake his hand followed by a few more of the men who knew him. Parsons noticed the usual group of tank topped biker bunnies sitting and chatting on two sagging well-worn corduroy couches in the next room waiting for their men to finish talking before being retrieved for another night of partying.

"Hi Joey. Glad you could make it. How was the ride?"

"Cold. What's up?"

"Here, have a drink."

"Merci. Why the summons?"

"Easy Joey. Are you carrying?"

"No. Look, what's going on?"

"Jack wants to see you."

Parsons threw down a short glass of cheap whiskey, burning all the down to his stomach. He turned to the office door at the rear of the room. The sign 'President' hung slightly slanted on a peg on the door. He waited a few seconds, put the glass on a table, walked to the rear and knocked on the door.

"Come in," a voice boomed from inside.

"Hi Jack. Hills said you want to see me."

Jacques Cote, known as Jack rose slowly, smiled widely and grabbed Parsons by the shoulders giving him a man hug. "So good to see you Joey. Sit down. Want a drink?"

"No thanks Jack." Parsons saw the one percent tattoo on his right forearm as Cote walked to the door and closed it. The tattoo was a badge of honour in the world of gangs and Cote was one of the bad of the bad.

"Jack, what is this all about?"

"Relax Joey. I just want to talk."

Parsons was not expecting what happened next. Cote sat back in his chair, lit a cigar and calmly proclaimed that the cocaine business was changing. The real money was now in street distribution, so it made more sense to buy the product from others who take the import risk, cut the strength and sell it to directly to street dealers. The organized crime folks that acted as middleman needed to be cut out. The decision had been made that there would be one more truck coming and one more sale to the buyers.

Parsons sat back a bit more relaxed. Why one more exchange Jack? If the decision is made, let's just do it."

"Joey, I need you to listen to this carefully. We have reason to believe that the mob is setting you guys up. We got wind the Feds have an informer and it is only a matter of time before they come down on us. We have always been concerned that the mob wants all the business without us transporting for them. They could be using the next transaction to take us down. My plan is to use that exchange to send a message to the mob that we are not stupid bikers and we protect our own."

Cote rose out of his chair and walked around his desk placing his hand on Parsons' shoulder.

"I am going to be straight. I can only trust you and the Skeletons with this."

Cote took a few long puffs of his cigar.

"Are you in?"

Parsons looked at Cote for a half minute thinking that beating up two guys from the mob wouldn't be a problem and overall, the plan to cut out the middleman was a good idea. "Yes Jack, I'm in."

"I knew I could count on you."Cote took a few more puffs on his cigar before giving Joey a strange look. "There is one other thing. Nate Thomas, how has he been lately?"

"Nate is Nate. Usually angry at the world, drinks too much, holds a grudge and needs a reminder every once in a while that we need to act as a team. Why do you ask?"

"Thomas is American and the tip we got was from one of our members in the States. I just don't like the coincidence."

Joey deliberately didn't respond and immediately returned to Cote's request. "So how do we avoid being set up at the next exchange?"

"Joey, you control when the product is brought into Canada and the time and location of the exchanges."

"How do you want to handle the last exchange with the mob?"

"Jack, I will have a plan. Give me a day or so."

"Good. Why not stick around here until you have the plan."

Parsons knew exactly what he meant so he called his house and told his girlfriend telling her that he was staying at the clubhouse overnight and would call in the morning.

After a restless night on a hard spare bed in the back of the clubhouse, Parsons woke to the sound of a few motorcycles revving up. Through the window, he could see two riders with their women taking off toward the city, no doubt on a shopping trip. Over his second cup of coffee, he had a plan to deal with the mob in his head.

Almost as if he knew, Cote walked through the kitchen and poured a coffee.

"Well? Anything for me Joey?"

"Yes. Let's go into your office."

Parsons laid out the plan in detail. He would advance the exchange two days and change the location to an open area near and old gas station on the highway. The day of the exchange, he would call the buyers in the afternoon and move the meeting from eight p.m. to five fifteen p.m., giving too little time for the authorities to set up. It would also be daylight so his men could see anyone else in the area.

"Jack, I need to know what you want me to do with the buyers."

"Simple. Tell Thomas to take them out. If he doesn't, we'll know who the informer is and deal with it."

"We?"

"You know what I mean. If he doesn't, you do it and take care of Thomas."

Parsons left the clubhouse within the hour, his mind moving a mile a minute and he never felt this level of agitation before. Even though he had a plan, he wasn't expecting the Thomas piece. The ride back was more uncomfortable.

October 12, 1976

"Brian, this was what I was afraid of. Even though Joey changed the day and time, the mob set us up. It must have been a real battle if Marcel was killed."

"It's bad Jack. Joey, Nate and Wally are in custody. The drugs and cash were confiscated."

"Was there any confirmation who killed the buyers?"

"No question. It was the Feds."

"How do you know?"

"Wally told our lawyer."

Jack Cote pursed his lips and pounded his desk. "Thomas. I knew it."

"Thomas?"

"Brian, I think he is an informer."

"Thomas? Jack, he has a long record."

"He sold out for whatever reason."

There was a silence before Brian spoke. "So if he was an informer, what do you want to do?"

"Let the courts deal with the charges against Wally, Joey and Thomas. If they are acquitted, we'll deal with Thomas before he can disappear. If they get jail time, we'll protect Wally and Joey and let it be known that Thomas is on his own."

"What about the clubhouse Jack?"

"Schedule two guys at the gate from dusk to dawn and make sure they're armed. No one goes out alone."

"Anything else?"

"Get some cash to the girls and tell them they can do what they want to do."

Chapter 2

Dr. Harold Fresher was in his office by 7:00 a.m. 1 April 1992. It was much earlier than usual thanks to his phone at home ringing an hour earlier with some prankish kid randomly dialing numbers. At least the boy had the politeness to say April Fools before he hung up. Getting back to sleep was impossible so Fresher shaved and enjoyed a long shower, then off to the office to catch up on some paperwork.

Sitting in front of his antique desk, with files in his hand and enjoying his second cup of morning coffee, he heard Samid arrive in the office.

"Harold, I am surprised to see you in so early. I could smell the coffee halfway down the block."

"Good morning Samid, just catching up on some administration. Is it still raining?"

"Yes and I am getting a bit tired of all the rain we have had in the past few days. I hate having to use an umbrella when I go for my daily walk. Let me refill the coffee pot."

Ten minutes later, Samid came back into his office.

"Harold, Detective Stiles is on the phone and wants to speak to you."

"At this hour of the day? It must be another April fool's joke. Put him through."

"Good morning Bill. I'm impressed. It's just after dawn. Starting your day off with the roosters, eh?"

"Never short for words are you Harold. Maybe one day I'll get a job like yours; you know regular hours and an assistant to make my coffee. It would sure beat being up all night getting soaked to the skin working an assault case."

"Is this an April fool's joke? "

"Nope. It's true."

"So, what happened?"

"A woman was accosted late last night on Garth Street."

"Any leads?"

Stiles laid out what he had so far. A city street sweeper was rounding the corner and saw a man holding a woman by the hair and slapping her. When the man saw the street sweeper, he jumped in a car and raced away. The worker gave the police a good description of the driver and the car; plain black late model sedan; partial plate number. The police had already run the information and the car was stolen earlier that evening.

"Why did you call me? Assault and a stolen car is a police matter. Is there something you need me to do to help?"

"It's the woman. She asked me if I knew a good private investigator. All the good ones are busy, so I called you." Stiles laughed before saying, 'April Fool'.

"Very funny Bill."

"Couldn't resist. Seriously, she asked for a PI. Her name is Mrs. Rosetta Masters. We took her to Hamilton General and they kept her overnight for observation. She is in room 414. The doctors advised that she would be released today."

"Bill, did she mention why she needed someone like me? You folks are handling the investigation."

"Not a clue. I asked her but she made it clear it wasn't a police matter."

Fresher hung up the phone and sipped the last of his coffee before putting his coat on.

"Samid, my car is in the shop again, can you call me a cab. I need to meet a prospective client at the hospital."

In the back of the taxi, he mulled over what Bill Stiles had told him. 'It wasn't a police matter'. How could it not be? She was assaulted. It must be something extra ordinary.

****

Fresher arrived at the hospital shortly after nine o'clock and exchanged pleasantries with the older red shirted volunteer on the information desk doing the daily crossword. The lobby was the usual flurry of activity with every elevator full of staff coming and going, deliveries and visitors.

Fresher exited the elevator on the fourth floor. It was a couple of years since he was on that ward but immediately recognized a few of the medical staff. The hustle and bustle never changes, he thought; patients and nurses going in and out of their rooms, visitors searching for the small glass walled waiting room, and the breakfast cleanup staff juggling trays. He made his way down the hallway to room 414 and entered slowly. It was a two patient room but only one bed was occupied and judging by the small bandage on the woman's hairline, she was Rosetta Masters. The doctor was just finishing attending to Masters' chart, telling her that he was discharging her and giving her a prescription for pain. The doctor left the room without a goodbye to his patient and passed Fresher at the door without acknowledging him. Typical bedside manner he thought.

Fresher was now completely in the room and could see that the woman was in her mid forties, thin with salt and pepper hair. She wasn't wearing any makeup and her face was as cold as stone. Her large dark eyes and full lips gave away her Italian heritage. Through all that, Fresher could see that she was what many men could consider somewhat attractive. Her features fit the first name Rosetta but not a surname like Masters. His trained eye noticed that she had no wedding ring, not even a tan line or a ring impression on her finger. He also stared briefly at a tattoo on her upper left breast as the hospital gown slipped while she was sitting back down on bed. It was a small pink hand of a skeleton. He couldn't recall ever seeing anything like it before.

"Mrs. Masters?"

"Who are you?"

"My name is Dr. Harold Fresher."

"What do you want? The other doctor just discharged me."

15

"I'm sorry Mrs. Masters, I should have explained. I have a doctorate in Investigative Process and have been practicing private investigating here in Hamilton for a few years. Detective Stiles called me this morning and said you would like to speak to a private detective. How can I help you?"

"Dr. Fresher, please close the door and sit down", she said curtly.

Masters sat on the edge of the bed, her rigid face focused directly at Fresher. In short, firm words she said, "Last night wasn't a random assault, and I was targeted."

"Did you tell the police that?"

"No."

"Don't you think that would have been a good idea?"

"No."

Fresher stared at Masters trying to comprehend what she was trying to say.

"Mrs. Masters, you will forgive me but I have been in this game for a long time and an assault is a very serious matter. The police are best equipped to handle these incidents. I really think that if you have any information that points to you as the target, you need to call Detective Stiles."

"No, Dr, Fresher. You need to understand why I believe I was the target and why I do not want the police involved."

Fresher rose from his chair and walked to the window contemplating what to do next. He turned toward the woman.

"Mrs. Masters before I can commit to helping you, I need details and I would like you to start from the beginning."

"Not here. Give me your business card and I will drop in tomorrow morning at 9:00a.m. I have a few things that need to be done today. Now if you'll excuse me so I can get dressed and get out of here."

Fresher stood in the hallway for a minute totally puzzled at the conversation with Masters. No question, she was a no nonsense woman and everything would be done on her schedule and that she truly believed she was targeted Fresher could not recall ever having to deal with a client with such a firm personality. Oh well he thought, he would listen to her and reserve any judgment until after their meeting.

As he stepped off the elevator on the main floor, stopped and a wide smile broke out on his face.

"Jenn."

"Hi Harold. Is everything okay? More stitches?" she asked slightly sarcastically.

"No Jenn, no more stitches." he replied with a slight grin on his face. I was just meeting a client."

"I bet it has something to do with the woman that was brought in last night."

"Very perceptive, but you know I can't get into it."

"Yes, I know. Hey, are we still on this weekend?"

"I wouldn't miss it. Pick you up at six thirty Saturday evening."

Jenn smiled and gave Fresher a full-extended hug before stepping onto the empty elevator. Inside, he wondered if his friendship with Jenn Gallager was becoming more than a weekend date.

He could still feel her arms around him and smell her perfume as he stepped into the taxi.

Chapter 3

At precisely 9:00 a.m. the next morning, Samid announced the arrival of Rosetta Masters. Fresher rose and extended his hand that she took briefly. Inconspicuously, he gave her a quick up and down look. He wasn't sure that it was the same woman he met in the hospital. Her hair was coiffed perfectly and the facial makeup took at least ten years off her age. The small bandage was only partially appearing under the hair. Her coat was a tailored London Fog and the outfit underneath was out of a fashion magazine. Her bracelet and neck chain were real gold and her left wrist sported a small face Tudor Rolex.

"Good morning Mrs. Masters, can I offer you a coffee?

"No thank you, I only have an hour. Can we get started?"

Fresher should have known that Masters was on a mission. He met this woman only once and didn't have a warm feeling then and today wasn't much better. In addition, the issue of her not wanting to involve the police, sent Fresher's defense mechanisms up. He was uncertain if she was going to become a client and he knew that this was the moment of decision.

"Certainly Mrs. Masters."

"Good, Dr. Fresher, let me tell ...."

Before she could start, Fresher jumped in. "Mrs. Masters, I think we need to start over. My work is predicated on honesty, a full disclosure and me asking questions. Are you okay with this?"

Rosetta Masters sat erect in her chair scowling at Fresher. He could see her mind processing what he said and fully expected her to get up and leave. The silence in the room extended well over a minute until Masters spoke.

"What do you need to know?"

"You told me in the hospital that you thought you were the target of the assault. Why do you feel that way?"

"It's a long story."

Normally, Fresher wanted clients to spend a few minutes and give him a feeling about their life. In Master's case, he needed to get to the crux of the matter as quickly as possible so he could decide whether to take on the case.

"Is there a short version?"

"Yes." As if she was reading off a list, she started. "Last week I received a letter from a lawyer that my brother Bruno left a Trust for me. It is valued at $625,000 and will be released once I sign a form. My brother was killed in a work accident in February 1982 and why the money sat in a Trust for ten years, I do not know. What is much more a concern is that there is no way that he could have that much money. He worked the docks in Halifax. He was a labourer, not some banker."

"Mrs. Masters, that is quite the story but it doesn't help me understand why you think you were the target last night."

"Dr. Fresher. There is more."

Looking down at her hands and squeezing her fingers, she slowly lifted her head and went on to tell Fresher that the same day she received the letter from the lawyer, she got a phone call from a man with a deep voice. He would not identify himself and told her 'he was coming after something she had'. She was convinced that the money and the call were connected.

"Did you recognize the deep voice?"

"No, but I knew he was serious."

"So you think that Bruno may have stolen the money from the man with the deep voice who then found out that you were getting it and then sent a message by assaulting you?"

Startled that Fresher had come to the same conclusion so quickly, she said, "Yes."

"Did the man that assaulted you say anything?"

"No. There wasn't time. As soon as the man grabbed me and hit me, the street sweeper came around the corner."

"Did you see his face?"

"No, it was dark and raining and it happened so fast. All I remember is that he had long blond hair."

"Mrs. Masters, that is quite the story and I can see why you think you are in danger, but again, I think you need to see the police."

"No, absolutely not."

"So, what do you want me to do?"

"Dr. Fresher, I would like you to find out whose money it is and arrange to give it back. I will be very honest with you. If the police get involved in this and the money is dirty, I don't want to be in danger or my brother's name to be dragged through the mud."

Fresher looked at Masters and let her words sink in. It was one thing to take the money, but to arrange to give it back to someone that roughs up women was not appealing. He stood up and walked to the window mulling over her request. Every instinct said to decline the case.

"Mrs. Masters, I want to understand this clearly. Your brother amassed a small fortune that you think was probably stolen. You think that whomever the money was stolen from has tracked you down. You want me to find that person and arrange to give the money back. Have I got that right?"

"Yes."

Fresher sat back down and stared at Masters. He made up his mind. "Mrs. Masters, this may not be an easy task, but if you are prepared to give me a four thousand dollar retainer, I will do my best."

Masters immediately reached into her designer purse. "Here is a cheque for the retainer. Call me when you have any information."

Rosetta Masters rose to leave. "Mrs. Masters, please sit down. We still have fifteen minutes left for your appointment and I need to know more about you and Bruno."

"What good will that do?"

"I have learned long ago that quite often the answers too many questions are in the past."

"Last year......"

"No, I would like you to go back, way back. Let's have the full version this time."

Fresher listened intently as Masters started at the beginning. She was born Rosetta Riso in Sudbury in 1949, three years after her brother Bruno. Her parents were Italian immigrants arriving soon after the war ended and because of the labour shortage in the mining industry in Canada, they were sent to Sudbury where he worked as a miner. Her mother worked as an office cleaner until the children came along. In 1957 after a long bought of pneumonia, she died. Rosetta was only eight years old and along with Bruno and her Dad, was thrown into a time of grief and uncertainty. Her brother was at the perfect age to pick up all the bad habits from the wrong crowd. Her father found solace in the bottle, becoming angry and abusive taking his temper out on both children. By the time Bruno was sixteen, he had enough of being a punching bag and left Sudbury in 1962 winding up in Halifax working as a long shore man. Rosetta was left alone to fend off her father's tirades and his attempts to seek sexual pleasure. In 1965, at age sixteen, she eloped to Toronto with a boy from school named Billy Masters. They both worked as packers in a typical manufacturing sweatshop, but the marriage lasted only six months when Masters decided he didn't want to be married anymore. He took off and she never saw him again. Later that year, she left for Calgary where she heard there was lots of work and reverted to her maiden name. Over the next eleven years, Rosetta Riso worked as a waitress and took bookkeeping courses at night. The winters were brutal and reminded her of Sudbury so in January 1977 she moved to Hamilton and took a job as a bookkeeper at one of the steel companies. She went back to her married name, Mrs. Rosetta Masters finding out that it fended off unwanted men. She was happy in Hamilton, enjoying a single lifestyle rebuilding her life, however, meager it was. Then everything changed last month when she received a letter from a lawyer in Toronto, the phone call, and the assault.

Fresher was intrigued by her use of the word, 'meager'. From her clothes and jewelry, she was living anything but a meager existence.

"Mrs. Masters, you said you had no idea that your brother set up a Trust for you. Did you not communicate with him when he was living in Halifax?"

"We wrote a couple of times a year. I sent letters to a post office box. He had my telephone numbers in Calgary and here and would call at Christmas. Other than that, we weren't that close."

"You also said he died in a work accident. Do you have any details?"

"In early 1982, I received a call from a man telling me he was my brother's Executor and that Bruno had been killed by a broken boom while unloading a ship. According to the initial investigation by the Safety Board, there was no sign of any tampering of the boom and it truly was an accident. He faxed me a copy of a newspaper article reporting on the accident that included a picture of Bruno. He also sent a copy of the death certificate. Now I realize that it may not have been an accident given the money in the Trust. The man said that as per Bruno's will, he was taking charge of the funeral and burial. I wanted to go to the funeral, but I was just getting grounded here so I made a promise to myself to visit his grave one day."

"I have a couple of more questions. Did the man mention any Trust?"

"No. I remember some of the call and there was no mention of a Trust."

"Did you ask about your brother's personal effects?

"No. I just assumed that Bruno being a labourer didn't have anything of value."

"Did you get the name of the man?"

"I don't remember his name or see anything in the papers the lawyer sent. Frankly, I didn't look the papers over very carefully."

"Did you by any chance happen to bring the letter from the lawyer?"

"Yes, I thought you might need to see it."

Masters handed the letter to Fresher who quickly made a copy and gave the original back to her.

"Mrs. Masters, please call me Harold. It may take me a few days to get answers. Until then, I suggest you try to stay in your home and away from places where there are crowds. I can arrange for security if you want."

"Dr. Fresher, I am not scared. I can take care of myself. I look forward to hearing from you."

Fresher heard, 'Dr. Fresher' even though he asked her to call him Harold. Masters rose from the chair, put on her coat and left without saying goodbye.

Fresher sat behind his desk realizing that the past twenty-four hours dropped an interesting case into his lap. Masters' connection of the money to the call seemed to be real but her refusal to take the threat seriously concerned him. Her idea of finding out whom the money was stolen from and giving it back was even more bizarre. Fresher knew that if the assault was a warning, it could escalate to a much higher degree of danger and therefore he needed to act quickly.

There was one more question that rolled around in Fresher's mind – how could a waitress turned bookkeeper live a seemingly rich lifestyle. She hadn't received the money from the Trust yet but had the financial resource to live the high life. He parked that in the back of his brain because the he needed to work quickly.

****

"Samid, what did you think of Mrs. Masters?"

"Quite the number; the makeup, the clothes, the jewelry, all high end stuff."

"Well, believe it or not, she is a bookkeeper at the steel plant. I took her case but something isn't right."

"You should have seen her car parked out front, a Mercedes no less."

"A Mercedes?"

"That explains why she didn't bat an eye writing that cheque for four thousand dollars."

"Harold, not sure if you noticed but the address on this cheque is one of Hamilton's luxury adult condominiums."

Fresher sat in his office late that morning reviewing Rosetta Masters' story. If the money was stolen by Bruno in 1982 or before, and was now in a Trust for Masters, how would the person that was robbed or cheated get information regarding the Master after so many years? To Fresher, there were only two possibilities. Either the unknown Executor or the lawyer must be implicated. He retrieved the letter from the lawyer and read it through twice before he noticed something unusual. The inheritance was in the name Rosetta Masters and Family. 'And Family', why would the document say, 'And Family'? Masters said nothing about a family. He saw no wedding ring and the condominium was an adult only building. He knew she was old enough to have been married, divorced and even have children that could be grown up by now. That was something he may need to look into.

The letter was from Marsha Milligan, a Toronto based lawyer. A good place to start, he thought so he called her office number and was surprised that Marsha Milligan answered he own phone. After explaining who he was and why he was calling, she readily agreed to see him first thing the next morning in her Toronto office.

****

As Fresher was wrapping up the day, Samid came in and told him that Rosetta Masters was on the phone and was quite agitated.

"Mrs. Masters, is everything all right?"

"Harold, I received another call. The voice was yelling at me that time had run out and he was coming for me."

Fresher caught the use of 'Harold'. "Was it the same voice as the first time?"

"Yes. It was deep and I somehow think it was American. Harold, I might need that security you offered."

For the first time, Fresher saw some vulnerability in Masters.

"Mrs. Masters, I'll arrange for two brothers named Wowchuk to check in on you in the next hour and give you a walkie-talkie. One will stay parked outside your building until we can find out what is going on. If he sees anything unusual or hears from you, the police will be there in minutes"

As soon as Fresher got off the phone, he relayed instructions to Samid to arrange for the Wowchuks.

Chapter 4

With his car still in the shop, Fresher was at the rental office waiting for it to open. He was anxious to get to Toronto and knew that the trip would be at least an hour given he had to locate Milligan's office, park, and walk.

At two minutes after 9:00 a.m., he walked through the door of a storefront office on the west side of Toronto.

"Hello Dr. Fresher I assume. Please come in."

"Thank you. Ms. Milligan?"

Fresher had seen many of these types of law offices before. There were several open cabinets marked by letters of the alphabet. On Milligan's desk was a pile of six or seven folders, and the corner of the room was stacked with boxes of old files. There was no sign of an assistant. He learned long ago that despite what looked like a bit of disorganization, lawyers were usually quite sharp and well on top of the cases they handled.

"Dr. Fresher, your reputation precedes you. I attended a few legal conferences over the years and your name often comes up as one of the industry's best investigators. I am honoured."

"Thank you Ms. Milligan. Please call me Harold."

"And, please call me Marsha. You mentioned on the phone that this relates to the Trust that was set up for Mrs. Rosetta Masters by her brother Bruno."

"Yes. His sister, Rosetta, is trying to understand how he was able to amass well over half a million dollars between the ages of sixteen and thirty-six. She fears that the money may have been accumulated illegally. I am trying to get more details for her."

Marsha Milligan looked at Fresher with a wide smile. "No, I seriously doubt that."

"You doubt that the money was gotten illegally?"

"Absolutely sure of it."

"Marsha, can you start at the beginning. I need to understand everything about Bruno and your relationship with him."

Milligan proceeded to lay out the entire story for Fresher. She graduated from St. Mary's in 1969 with a law degree specializing in Trusts and Estates. Bruno Riso was one of her first clients. He walked into her office the second week she was in business and gave her a cheque for $12500 asking her to set up a Trust for his sister. He would come in every five or six months and give her cheques, some quite large. She asked once about where the money came from and he told her it was wise investing. He always took the time to name his investments and it was clear that he knew what he was talking about. Even after she moved her practice to Toronto, he continued to travel from Halifax to see Milligan and provide more money. This happened until he died.

"This doesn't make sense Marsha. He was a labourer on the docks in Halifax. He was unionized and these guys don't make that kind of money."

"Labourer? I don't think so. Every time I saw him, he was dressed impeccably. I know well dressed men from my profession. Custom monogrammed shirts, hand stitched suits, silk ties and Italian leather shoes. He had it all including the Rolex. His cheques were personalized and his address where I sent quarterly statements was one of the premier buildings in Halifax."

Fresher sat in disbelief. "Are we talking about the same man? This is unbelievable."

"Let me pull the file. Here it is. Over the course of our thirteen year professional relationship, he deposited nearly $175,000 into the Trust. An additional $210,000 came in from his estate. He also gave me very explicit instructions how the money was to be invested even if and when something should happen to him. The Trust finalized with a sixty-one percent return. The final number of six hundred and twenty five thousand is net of any legal fees."

Fresher sat speechless for several seconds. His mind was rapidly going through the complications and different truths of the case.

"Marsha, why was there a ten year delay in releasing the Trust?"

"I have no idea. That was Bruno's wish and my duty was to comply with it."

"How did you find out he died?"

"I received a letter with a copy of the death certificate and Bruno's Last Will and Testament from Bruno's Executor, a man named Barry Holstead."

"Do you know who this Holstead is?"

"No, however, I noticed in Bruno's will, he and Holstead lived in the same building. I assumed they were good friends."

"Marsha, the Trust is made out to 'Rosetta Masters and Family'. Was that how it was started?"

"No. Mr. Riso added 'And Family' in 1979. I didn't ask why as it was none of my business. All I remember is he was concerned that something may happen to his sister and any family she had should get the money."

"Marsha, this isn't meant to offend you but was there anyone else that might have had knowledge of the Trust and the distribution to Bruno Riso's sister beside you?"

"No, Harold, as you can see, I am a one person operation. The only other persons would have been the bank and the Canada Revenue Agency. I would think that the Executor may also know if Mr. Riso confided in him."

"Would it be possible to get Mr. Riso's address in Halifax?"

As Milligan was writing out the address, her eyes squinted at Fresher.

"Harold, you mentioned illegal activity and I am getting a sense that this Trust may be causing Mrs. Masters some grief. Anything I can do?"

"No Marsha. It's complicated and frankly, there is an element of risk for anyone that knows too much."

Fresher left Milligan's office with more information that he thought he would get, and more questions than he wanted.

****

Fresher made it back to Hamilton shortly after noon and stopped by to talk to the Wowchuk brother that was on duty.

"Hi Gene. Anything happening?"

"Everything is quiet Dr. Fresher. I took over from my brother Garth this morning and checked in with Mrs. Masters. All is well."

Fresher proceeded to his office. The door was locked so he knew Samid was gone for lunch. As he was opening the door, he felt a poke in his back and heard a deep male voice.

"Don't turn around. Get your nose out of my business. This has nothing to do with you. I won't be so gentle if I have to come back."

Fresher saw the opportunity. "How much money do you want from Rosetta Masters?"

"This has nothing to do with money."

With that, the man pushed Fresher hard through the door causing Fresher to stumble to the floor. Fresher got up and immediately went into his office and looked out the window. Across the street, a white pickup was quickly pulling away from the curb. All Fresher could see was the back of a man's head with long blond hair.

As soon as Samid returned, Fresher told him about the confrontation and asked him to keep the camera ready instructing him to go into the back file room every half hour, peek through the blinds to the street out front and if a white pickup with a blond male driver was parked, take pictures.

Fresher also asked Samid to let the Wowchuks know that in all likelihood, Masters was in danger by a blond man in a white pickup truck. If they saw him, try to get pictures.

"Harold, are you sure you don't want me to call the police?"

"No, Samid. I do think that guy is after Rosetta Masters and may harm her but there is nothing that we can offer the police that would substantiate what I suspect. Besides, the Wowchuks are on it."

A half hour later, the phone rang in Fresher's office. It was Gene Wowchuk.

"Dr. Fresher, I saw the blond guy in the white pickup a few times this morning. He got out once and tried to go in the building but didn't have the code. Anyway, I have some pictures for you. He saw me with the camera and took off in a hurry. Garth is on his way to relieve me so I'll drop the film of in a half hour."

Samid was waiting at the door for Wowchuk, took the film immediately, slipped out the back door and walked quickly to the one-hour photo shop three blocks away. An hour and a half later, he returned with copies for Fresher. The photos came out very clear, clear enough that he was able to fax a copy to Detective Stiles with a request to run the photo through the files and see if there was a match.

Before leaving his office, he called Masters that he was stopping by on his way home. She gave him the entry code.

It was the first time that he had been in this building and the lobby was something out of a magazine. The marble, the glass, the upscale furnishings were indicative of a seriously expensive building.

Fresher's second knock on her door was answered and he walked into a residence filled with the finest furniture and appointments. Everything went together as if it had been professionally decorated. Even the artwork fit in and Fresher thought he wouldn't be surprised if the paintings were originals.

"Mrs. Masters. I wanted to pop by and give an update."

"Thank you. I must say that those Wowchuk boys are attentive. They are big boys and I feel a lot safer with them around. Thank you for arranging for them."

Fresher took a few minutes telling Masters that he met with Marsha Milligan. Bruno gave her large sums of money every few months and when he died, that money as well as his cash assets went into a Trust. The money was the result of wise investing, investing that Milligan was convinced to be true. Fresher commented that Milligan was given very specific investment instructions in Bruno's will and there was a directive not to release the Trust for ten years but he didn't know why.

"Mrs. Masters, there was something very unusual. Bruno actually delivered the money to Milligan in person a few times. According to her, your brother was anything but a labourer on the docks. He wore the finest tailor made clothes and expensive jewelry."

Fresher could see that Masters was struggling to understand. "My brother? That can't be. I saw the article in the paper."

"Mrs. Masters, I may need to go to Halifax to speak with Bruno's Executor. I was also able to get Bruno's address and would like to talk with any of the neighbours that are still there."

Masters nodded her head in agreement, still trying to fathom what Fresher said about her brother.

"Mrs. Masters, there is one other thing. You told me that the man that called you said,' he was coming after something you had' and we just assumed it was the money. I am not sure that the two issues are related."

"Why would you say that Dr. Fresher?"

Fresher told Masters that a blond man seen trying to get into her building was the same man that threatened him and that was too much of a coincidence. In addition, the man made it very clear to Fresher that money wasn't what he wanted.

"Mrs. Masters, we were able to get a photo of the man. Here, do you recognize him? Is he the same man that assaulted you?"

Masters took the picture and looked at it for at least fifteen seconds. Fresher could see her eyes widen before returning to normal. She handed the picture of the blond man back to Fresher and quickly nodded 'no'.

"Mrs. Masters, as I said, I don't think the money and the threats are linked. I would suggest that I put off my trip to Halifax until the man in the picture explains what he is doing."

Fresher got up and headed for the door when he stopped and turned around.

"Mrs. Masters, there is one other thing. Why would your brother change the beneficiary of the Trust from you, to you 'And Family'?"

Masters shrugged her shoulders indicating that she had no idea and walked away.

Chapter 5

The following morning, Fresher checked in with one of the Wowchuks. Everything was okay at Masters' condominium and there were no more sightings of the blond man or the white pickup truck. His next call was to Stiles.

"Hi Bill. Did you get my fax?"

"Yes, Harold. Where did you get this picture?

"He's part of a case I am working on. It seems he wants something from my client."

"Does this have anything to do with the woman who was assaulted a few days ago, the woman that wanted the PI?"

"Yes."

"Well, you really know how to pick them."

"So, he has a record?"

"More than a simple record."

"You sound serious."

"Very, in fact I asked the Calgary police to fax me a file that involves this character."

Stiles laid it out. The blond man was Nathan Michael Thomas, an American. He had been in and out of custody since he was a teenager largely in North Dakota. One of the charges was manslaughter, but he was a minor then and served only a year in juvenile detention. There was a gap in years until October 1976 when he was arrested south of Calgary for drug smuggling and money laundering both sides of the Canada –USA boarder. According to the file, he was part of a small four-member team from a motorcycle gang called Dark Destiny. There were three others - Parsons, Orte and Bowen. The four called themselves the Skeletons. Stiles went on to tell Fresher that the file notes painted Dark Destiny as very serious characters. The Skeletons took on special work; in this case, it was drug smuggling. There was more. All four met a transport truck near the Roseville/Grasmere border crossing and transferred sixty pounds of uncut, pure cocaine into their saddlebags. They drove fifty miles north and met two men. A combined Canada-USA team of border agents set up an ambush to nail the bikers and the buyers. Gunfire ensued and one biker and two other men were shot dead. Three were arrested. Thomas was sentenced to fourteen years and was deported on his release. I checked on him and he was arrested upon leaving prison here and served another two years in the States for an old outstanding charge. He was recently released but never checked in with his parole officer and a warrant was issued.

"Harold, do you think this Thomas character is the person that assaulted the woman?"

"I'm sure of it."

"Well, regardless, if this guy is in Canada with an outstanding warrant from the States, he is in big trouble."

"Yes, I figured that out. Bill, you said a combined Canada-USA team of border agents. How would they get the information?"

"The file has notes going back several months before the arrests but I can tell that there are pieces missing. That's to be expected in these old files. Harold, let's get back to Thomas. This is a bad dude. You need to tell me what is going on."

"To be honest, I am not sure yet. Give me a few days and I'll tell you all I have. Listen, before you go, do you have Thomas' mug shot from his arrest?"

"Yes. I'll fax it over."

"Bill, leave it in an envelope at the front desk of the station and I will pick it up. Oh, and one more thing, does the report say anything about who the other two dead men were?"

"The file photos show that they were dressed in suits and ties. They were known to police as part of the mob and it would be good guess that they were buyers."

"How does the report finish?"

"The last page is a list of the drugs and cash found at the scene. There was sixty pounds of cocaine and $175,000."

"$175,000 doesn't seem like much for sixty pounds of coke."

"That would have been the going rate back then."

****

After he picked up the envelope, Fresher sat in the car looking at the mug shot. He wasn't surprised to see it match the photo from Wowchuk.

Yes, Thomas was quite a few years younger in the mug shot, but the facial features and the hair were the same.

With a hat pulled low and sunglasses on, Fresher drove past his office on the way to see Masters. There was no pickup truck. In the parking lot of the condominium, he took another look at the mug shot. Thomas was holding the identification plate in front of him but Fresher's eyes saw something else, the tattoo of a skeleton's hand on his lower right arm. It was the same skeleton hand tattoo he saw on Rosetta, except Thomas' tattoo was black ink.

****

Fresher checked in with Garth Wowchuk before going up to Masters' suite.

"Hi Garth. Anything happening?"

"No Harold. All quiet. I thought you were going to Halifax?"

"Change of plans Garth."

After hearing two knocks on the door and an eye through the peephole, Masters nervously opened the door ushering Fresher quickly inside. He was once again impressed with the suite and its contents. He stood until Masters motioned him to a chair. Fresher could see that the delay in getting answers for her was taking its toll.

Fresher sat down resolved that he wasn't going to leave until he knew what she knew. He remembered the quick, 'no' when he asked her about the blond man but there was the skeleton's hand issue - that couldn't be a coincident.

"Mrs. Masters, I am going to be blunt. Why is Nate Thomas after you?"

Rosetta Masters stiffened in her chair, both eyes focused on Fresher.

"Who is Nate Thomas?" she said defensively.

Fresher showed her the mug shot and could see that he hit a nerve.

"This is Nate Thomas, right? It's the same person I showed you before, except in this one he is much younger."

Before she could answer, there was a knock on the door. Fresher was startled. He jumped out of his chair and looked through the peephole. It was Garth Wowchuk.

"Harold, that blond man in the pickup truck is parked a block away from the here. He has his eyes glued on the front door. What do you want me to do?"

"Nothing." Fresher picked up the phone and called Detective Stiles telling him Thomas was parked near Masters' building.

"Garth, head back downstairs and keep an eye on the pickup. As soon as the police and have Thomas in custody, come back up."

In thirty minutes, Wowchuk was knocking on the door.

"They have him in custody, Harold. I watched the whole thing unfold and have to hand it to Detective Stiles."

Wowchuk went on to tell Masters and Fresher that the arrest process was flawless. Two female officers dressed casually strolled down the sidewalk. They knew Thomas would check them out then return his attention to the front door of the building. As soon as he did, both officers pulled out their service revolvers and pointed them at Thomas while three cruisers came around the corner and boxed in the white pickup truck. Thomas got out of the truck with fists clinched hesitating briefly, obviously pondering whether to go for the gun under his pant waistband. He heard Stiles yell, 'Don't do anything stupid Thomas. Cuff him.' Thomas resisted initially, but saw there was no way out. He was taken into custody.

"Dr. Fresher, it looks like the threat for Mrs. Masters is over. Do you still need my brother and me?"

"No, thank you Garth. I really appreciate your brother and you being available and so professional. I'm sure we'll do business again. Send me your bill."

As soon as Wowchuk left, Fresher and Masters sat down in opposite chairs. Fresher paused for a few seconds,

"Mrs. Masters, what is going on and no lies. Your brother was leading a double life, a labourer by night and a stock wizard by the day. Then, Thomas stalked you looking for something you have, and isn't the money. Thomas has the same skeleton's hand tattoo on his arm that you have on your chest. You were assaulted and I have been threatened. How are these things related? I want all of the truth. I cannot help you if there are any secrets."

"How did you know about my tattoo?"

"I saw it when you were in the hospital."

"Harold, would you like a drink? You may need it." It was the first sign of pleasantry that Fresher saw from his client.

Masters' face relaxed and she related a new version to her life's story. Everything up to her move to Calgary was true. About six years after her move west, she was waitressing one evening in a restaurant just off the highway outside of Calgary. A couple of bikers came in. They weren't noisy or rude, they just wanted some dinner. There was one man in particular that caught her eye. He was very good looking, was mannerly and took the time to talk to her rather than just ask for a date. His name was Joey Parsons.

Fresher became more interested in her story. Parsons, the name Parsons; that was the guy that Stiles mentioned in the report.

Fresher let Masters continue without any indication that he heard about Parsons.

Masters said that over the next few months, Joey came in almost every two weeks, sometimes with the others and sometimes by himself. Eventually, he asked her out and the rest is history. At twenty-two, she fell deeply in love with him and became what the other guys like to describe as, 'his biker bunny'. She quit her job and moved to a large house that four of the gang lived in. They called themselves the Skeletons and besides Parsons, there was Thomas, Bowen and Orte.

Fresher immediately recognized the other names from Stile's information.

Masters went on to tell Fresher that there were two other girls in the house, Jill and Mandy. One of the four men, Bowen, didn't have a steady girl preferring to play the field with one of several bar flies in the places he frequented. The men kept the women in clothes, food and good times. There was always the chance that one of the men would get drunk and rowdy, but it was Joey that calmed things down. She knew that the men were not on the right side of the law, but she loved Joey and dreamed of a time when he would leave the gang and take her with him. Everything was going well until late September 1976. The men left one morning. They didn't say where they were going, but Joey told her that they would be back in a day or two. She remembered that day very well because he left behind his medication.

"Medication?"

"Joey was taking something for a muscle twitch. It bothered him so badly, that he went to a doctor. None of the others knew."

Masters continued telling Fresher that the morning after the day they left, the police raided the house, arrested the women and several officers did a complete search. In jail, the women were told that Joey and two others, Nate and Wally had been arrested the previous afternoon and charged with attempted murder, smuggling, possession of a controlled substance and money laundering. Marcel Orte was shot and killed. The women were interrogated all the next day, but released being told that there was no evidence that they were implicated in the crimes. Their lawyer confided that the case against the men was quite complicated and the prosecution really didn't have the time to pursue the women's charges. As soon as the girls were back in the house, one of the gang showed up and gave each of them $200 and told to the girls to take off if they wanted but they stayed.

She tried to reach Joey for over two weeks, but could not get past the desk sergeant in the Calgary jail. It was during that time that she found out she was pregnant.

Fresher sat trying not to look surprised, but was having difficulty trying to absorb all of the information she was offering.

"Being pregnant was something I never expected. Joey was adamant that we use protection. It didn't matter how much we drank, it was protection or nothing. I told him more than once that I loved him, and he said he loved me, but we never talked about marriage or having children."

Masters said that the next several weeks were a blur. The gang was providing financial support but the girls were scared of what might eventually happen to them. The police came back to search the house several more times, and the press included pictures and names. The other two girls decided to leave. She told no one about the pregnancy.

Masters eyes became red and she dabbed them with a tissue before continuing. Christmas was coming and all the plans that Masters and Parsons had were now just memories. Masters was confused, concerned and conflicted as to what to do.

"I went to their trial every day and able to slip Joey a note through the public defender that I was pregnant. I recall him not even opening the note, just crumpling it and leaving it on the table. I was so upset. Midway through the fourth day in late December, the case wrapped up. The evidence was overwhelming and the defense had little to argue. Because the drug trafficking and money laundering occurred in both countries, sentences were severe. The judge sentenced Joey, Nate and Wally to fourteen years. When they were led away in handcuffs, Joey didn't even look my way. She heard that the US authorities tried to extradite Nate but they would need to wait until he served his sentence in Canada.

"I continued to try and reach Joey but the police and the public defender wouldn't talk to me. In the end that really didn't matter. "

"Why didn't it matter?"

"Joey died his first day in prison. I found out about it in a newspaper article just after New Year's Day. I received a copy of the newspaper article from a friend. According to the paper, he was in a fight and was knifed. Joey, who they described as a convicted drug dealer, died on route to the hospital. Only once did they mention Joey's name in the entire article. I cried the whole day."

Fresher made a mental note to talk to Stiles about Parson's death.

"Did you go to Parsons' funeral?"

"I called one of Joey's friends at the big club and was told that the death was over a week ago and Joey was buried by the province. I guess that is what happens when there is no next of kin."

"No next of kin?"

"None. We used to talk about a life together and he told me more than once he was orphaned very young and bounced around from foster parent to foster parent until he took to the road."

"I'm so sorry Mrs. Masters. It must have been a horrible time for you. Where is your child?"

Masters' put her head down, hesitated slightly and responded.

"In late January 1977, I was looking for a job in Calgary. Snow was coming down and I slipped off a curb, hit by a car and lost the child in the hospital. I was only slightly injured and was able to leave the hospital in two days."

Fresher was surprised that there wasn't more regret in Masters when she talked about the child.

"Mrs. Masters, this still didn't answer my question. Do you know of any reason that Thomas would be looking for you?"

Masters hesitated and lowered her eyes.

"Honestly, I don't have any idea what it could be. Joey is dead and I was just one of the girls."

Fresher's head was beginning to ache from all the information from Masters and he needed to shift. "Well Mrs. Masters, with the Thomas threat out of the way, I need to concentrate on Bruno and the money. I will be going to Halifax tomorrow."

As Fresher was driving home, questions after question gnawed at him. Why would Masters cry over the death of the man she loved yet showed very little grief over the loss and their child? Why, after so many years, would Thomas track her down with an issue so serious that he threatened Masters? Unfortunately, with Thomas back in custody, it was unlikely that anyone would ever know. It also concerned him that Masters wasn't always truthful. It was, however a relief that the only mystery now was the source of Bruno Riso's money.

Chapter 6

Later that morning, Fresher left for Halifax. The questions he had about Masters still rattled around in his head making the flight feel shorter. Once off the plane, he headed directly to Bruno Riso's building, the same one where Holstead lived.

The taxi pulled up in the front door of the middle of three eleven story older buildings nestled on a small court off Barrington Street. There was no mistaking that the enclave reeked of money. The well maintained grounds were dotted with high end vehicles parked on freshly paved parking spaces. The address that Milligan gave him for Holstead was Penthouse 2 and Bruno's unit 1006, one floor below. Fresher could see that the top floor units would feature spectacular views of the harbour.

As soon as he got out of the cab, he could see a glass wall fronting the entire main floor and inside a marble desk with a custodian sitting behind it. He was dressed in a typical doorman's uniform scanning several small monitors on the desk. Fresher entered the lobby and the man looked up and smiled. His name badge read,' William' and he looked like he had been there since the building was built.

"Good afternoon Sir, may I help you?"

"Yes, I am looking for Mr. Barry Holstead."

"I am sorry Sir, didn't you hear? Mr. Holstead passed away three years ago."

"No I didn't know."

Fresher's face drained thinking that he may have hit a hard dead end.

"William, my name is Dr. Harold Fresher." He hoped that pulling out the doctor title would help him. "I represent the family of a man named Bruno Riso."

"Oh, Mr. Riso. What a shame. Such a nice young man. He was a real gentleman and very well liked by the ladies. He was always impeccably dressed and so polite."

Fresher could see that William was a talkative kind and let him go on without interrupting.

"Mr. Riso was on the tenth floor overlooking the inner harbour. We often chatted about the navy ships that came in and out of port. He particularly liked to see visiting American craft coming into refuel. As he said, 'there was a certain magnificence about ships flying the red, white and blue'."

Fresher kept smiling and hoping that William would continue.

"I used to speak with Mr. Riso's cleaning team that came weekly. They loved working in his suite. There was so little work for them because he kept the place neat and tidy. I could tell you the habits of every tenant but I don't think that would be appropriate, if you know what I mean. One of my monitors is in the parking garage and I would see his two vehicles, one a new Lincoln that looked like it was hand washed every day; it was so shiny. He only used it on the weekends. His daily driver was a plain Ford F150 pickup a few years old. He never forgot me at Christmas. There was always an envelope, and always generous. He was with us for around fifteen or sixteen years. A real loss, he was. Funny you should also be asking about Mr. Holstead. The two of them were quite close. I would see them every few weeks or so coming back from a late lunch. Everybody misses both men."

Fresher had to steer the discussion. "William, do you know where Mr. Holstead worked?"

"Everyone did. He was with Lichten Investments on Upper Robie St. I bet half the residents in this building used him for financial advice. I even made a few bucks on his tips"

"What about Mr. Riso. Did he ever mention what he did for a living?"

"No, he never mentioned it to me but I did hear more than once that people thought he came from old money and was how do they say it, born with a silver spoon in his mouth. I was stunned when I read he was killed on the docks. The word was that he must have been an importer checking on a shipment."

"Was there anyone else in the building that Mr. Riso appeared to be close to?"

William let out a polite laugh. "Oh, yes. Miss Jamison on the fourth floor was his favourite. She is at least thirty years older than Mr. Riso and he was always taking her shopping or helping her with her chores. She is in a wheelchair and so enjoyed having Mr. Riso around. It was almost like a mother-son relationship."

"You said 'is' in a wheelchair?"

"Yes, she still lives here."

Fresher pounced on this information. "Is she in?"

"No. Today is her library day. She usually returns around four."

"Thank you William. You have been very helpful."

Fresher took the front desk telephone number from William and hailed a taxi. He hadn't been in Halifax for a couple of years and the trip to the Lichten offices reminded him how beautiful the city really was in late spring. The trip past a greening Citadel Hill, a glimpse of the old train station, going through the tree lined streets with stately houses on each side, all resurrecting good times of a younger man. The east end Lichten office was in an exquisitely refurbished century house near St. Mary's University. It was a small building with two cars in a driveway that was wide enough for four cars. Fresher admired the new Porsche beside a fairly new Cadillac. The front door of the building featured the original tall and wide stained glass window and an antique brass twist dinger. A small tasteful sign said, 'Please Enter'. He opened the door and walked in. There was and large hand carved antique oak desk with a teacher's desk bell and a sign, 'Please ring for service'. After one touch of the bell, a grey balding man holding reading glasses in one hand came into the room.

"Can I help you?"

"My name is Dr. Harold Fresher and I am representing the family of Bruno Riso. I believe he was a client of one of your employees, Barry Holstead."

"Doctor Fresher?" he asked with the emphasis on doctor.

"I can see what you are thinking. Here is my business card. I have a PhD in Investigative Process."

The man took the card, put his glasses on and looked at the words carefully before taking the glasses off and smiling at Fresher. "My name is Patrick Russell. Barry was my partner before his passing. He was a real asset. Listen, come into my office and have a coffee and we can chat."

Behind Russell's desk was a sign.

There are three ways to make money

The Right Way

The Wrong Way

The Other Way

Fresher could see that Patrick Russell was a very successful man. Not only were his clothes tailor-made and hand stitched, his Audemar Piguet watch complimented his diamond-studded cufflinks. No doubt, the Porsche in the driveway was his.

The office had an old oak smell with a classic hunter green area carpet on top of thin pine planked flooring. All the furniture was well cared for antiques. On the sidewalls were two small Kreigoffs. Russell saw Fresher looking at the paintings and offered that they were reproductions.

"Nice, aren't they? The originals are in his house."

Fresher immediately formed an opinion about Russell, that being he was a bit pompous.

"That is a very unique sign behind you Mr. Russell. Does it have any special meeting?"

"Yes, it does. The right way is for those that work for a living; the wrong way is for those that steal it; the other way is letting others make money for you, and that Sir is my business. So Dr. Fresher, what can I do for you?"

"Mrs. Rosetta Masters, Mr. Riso's sister, has retained me to look into the details of a Trust left to her. She is not refuting the Trust, but would like to bring closure as to the origin of the money. I know that Mr. Holstead worked here and was hoping that you may be of some assistance."

"Let me see what I have in the file."

The next hour was spent reviewing Holstead's file on Bruno Riso. Riso opened an investment account in late 1966. Riso's application gave Holstead complete authority on the investment strategy. The first deposit was $5000 cash. Riso had hit the market at a perfect time. There was a twenty-two percent loss in the stock market in 1966, but the recovery was substantial and anyone that got in at the bottom enjoyed unprecedented profits. Holstead knew the markets very well and made a phenomenal amount of money for himself and his partner over the years. Hiring a person like Holstead to know when to be a bull and when to be a bear cost the clients six percent of annual return on investment, but the clients didn't balk considering their returns were extremely substantial. The file did list Riso's profession as an employee of the Halifax Shipyard, and next of kin

Mrs. Rosetta Masters. A couple of years later, Marsha Milligan was added as his attorney. The account was closed in 1982 after Bruno's death and the balance of the investment account of $149,000 forwarded to the lawyer. It all seemed quite simple.

"Dr. Fresher, as you probably know, we were obligated to transfer his investment balance to the Trust that his lawyer was managing. I recall that Barry also transferred the cash assets to the lawyer as well. I knew that Barry was Riso's Executor and had the will secured in our company vault. I think he threw it out about eight or nine years after Riso's death. I remember Barry telling me that the will was very straightforward. There were two beneficiaries. One was one of my clients, Miss Jamison who was to receive $25,000, and the second was the Trust account for his sister. He also told me that Mr. Riso requested that the investment account balance and the Trust were not to be disclosed to Mrs. Masters. That was a strange request, but it wasn't up to an Executor to challenge the last will and testament of the deceased. It was pretty simple according to Barry."

"Mr. Russell, what would have been considered a good annual return during the years Mr. Riso was a client?"

"Between nine and twelve percent. Keep in mind that there were risks in the market, but Barry had a real knack of avoiding the losses."

"Is there anything on the files that indicate Mr. Riso's investment or profit?"

"Nothing. We only keep basic client information past seven years. We follow the law and shred all investment details."

Fresher left Patrick Russell with some solid answers. There was no doubt that Riso saved the initial investment in the first two to three years he was working; dockworkers were unionized and they often pulled a lot of overtime. He then befriended Holstead that helped Riso make his money through wise investing and established a Trust for his sister. He also understood the disclosure demands in the will requesting secrecy of the money for ten years. Things were falling in place quite nicely.

His next stop was to check into the hotel and have lunch. Over a club sandwich, Fresher jotted some numbers on the napkin. At the time of Bruno's death, the total received by Marsha Milligan was $210,000 yet Russell said that there was only $149,000 in the investment account. That meant that Bruno had over $60,000 cash on hand. Fresher quickly realized that living in Halifax in 1960's and 1970's would be pretty luxurious with that much cash on hand and the amount that his investments were making.

Fresher's was positive that the money was clean, based on excellent investment advice and diligent Trust management. He knew Masters would be satisfied with his findings, and somewhat comforted that the money was not stolen from someone else. He still had a few questions to answer so he could satisfy his own curiosity.

****

At four thirty, he was back at Riso's condominium standing in front of William.

"Dr. Fresher, welcome back."

"Hello William. I was wondering if Miss Jamison has returned."

"Yes, she has and I mentioned to her that one of Mr. Riso's friends was by earlier."

"Can you buzz her and ask her if she would have a few minutes for me."

Fresher went up to Miss Jamison's unit on the sixth floor. She was waiting with a small pure white Bichon Frise on her lap and a pot of tea and a plate of cookies on the coffee table. Fresher was impressed that a woman in a wheelchair could have refreshments ready only a few minutes after William announced that he was coming up.

"Dr. Fresher. William tells me that you were a friend of Bruno's. He was such a prince. If I were thirty years younger, I would have done anything to lasso that boy. What can I do for you? Did you want to give me a physical?" Williams' eyes twinkled with that remark and Fresher hoped he was that sharp when he got to her age.

"Miss Jamison, I am not a medical doctor. I am private investigator here on behalf of Bruno's sister."

Williams didn't react to the mention of Bruno's sister. Fresher knew that this woman knew a lot about Riso.

"I know he has been gone ten years, but there are a few questions she needs answers to so she can bring closure."

Fresher marveled at the bubbly personality that Miss Jamison displayed. He knew many older people that looked at aging as a time to be miserable. This woman could give lessons on being alive. He sipped his tea and explained he was wrapping up his report and was hoping that Miss Jamison could help him with the final pieces of information.

As she poured, each of them a second cup of tea, Fresher asked her if she knew what Riso did for a living and was prepared to hear something like banker or lawyer. Instead, Miss Jamison looked at Fresher with a coy smile on her face.

"Dr. Fresher. Every man has a skeleton in the closet. In Bruno's case, he came from a meager background where he had lost his mother and had an abusive father and had only occasional contact with his sister."

Fresher was surprised that she knew this much.

"Bruno swore me to secrecy."

"Well, Miss Jamison, he is gone now and I can assure you that I am bound to confidentiality as a private detective. I will tell his sister only what you say I can tell her."

That seemed to give Jamison the go ahead to tell all. Jamison met Bruno in 1963 in a supermarket. They would see each other every Tuesday early afternoon when Jamison and Bruno were on the same shopping schedule. Bruno would always help her with the bags to the taxi. Several months later, she asked him to have coffee with her. This became a ritual for almost two years. Bruno explained he was a dockworker, his background and that he had a dream of living a life of luxury. At that time, he had a small apartment on the west side. He told her that he had saved over $5000 and was hoping to parlay it into more. Jamison was delighted to introduce him to Barry Holstead and the rest was history.

"But that doesn't explain how he actually lived a double life."

Jamison poured more tea and looked like a Cheshire cat waiting to pounce.

"Well, as you said, poor Bruno is gone so I guess I can tell you. He moved into this building in 1966. His shift was six pm to two a.m., Sunday through Thursday. Before he left for work, he always took my dog for a walk, rain or shine. He would leave at five thirty in the afternoon in his pickup truck dressed casually and change at work then back to casual to return home. Everyone except Barry and I thought he had a lady friend and was with her each night. I would always ask him why he continued to work on the docks. He told me that it made him feel needed and kept him in shape. I believed him."

Fresher sipped more of his tea smiling inside.

"You know Dr. Fresher, Bruno left me $25,000 in his will. I really didn't need it, so I gave it all to the Nova Scotia Humane Society."

Jamison spent the next half hour relating anecdotes about Bruno. She often accompanied him to his tailor to pick out suit material and even chose the colour of his new Lincoln. Fresher got the feeling that Jamison was Bruno's soul mother.

"Miss Jamison, was there a love interest in Bruno's life?"

With that, Jamison let out a loud laugh. "Oh, no Dr. Fresher. He told me that I was the love of his life."

Fresher joined in the laughter before he continued. "I am assuming that his job and investments were his only income."

"Dr. Fresher, Bruno was as honest as the day is long. Take it from an old girl that knows people very well, he was the real deal, so to speak."

"Miss Jamison, I have one more question if you have time.

"I have all the time in the world."

"Did Bruno's sister have a family?"

"He never mentioned a family. I know she spent time in Calgary then moved east, but there was no talk of a husband or children.

"Miss Jamison, you have been so helpful, and with the tea and cookies, I won't have to eat until tomorrow."

"It has been my pleasure Dr. Fresher. Please drop by next time you're in Halifax."

Fresher returned to his hotel where he enjoyed a fresh lobster dinner before retiring to his room and finishing his notes for Masters. He was pleased that the money was accumulated honestly. He still had some nagging questions such as how Masters was able to live her lifestyle on an accountant's salary and what this Nate Thomas issue was all about, but the lifestyle was none of his business and Thomas was out of the picture.

Chapter 7

Before Fresher boarded the early Friday morning flight back to Toronto, he made a quick call to Samid asking him to invite Masters to his office early afternoon. He didn't want to tell Masters by telephone; he wanted to see her face when he told her that Bruno's money was legally attained and was invested and given in good faith. Deep down, he wished he knew a Barry Holstead and that there were still big money to be made with a meager investment.

As the plane approached the airport in Toronto, there was a light dusting of spring snow on the ground. He didn't know why, but it brought Jenn Gallager to mind. Maybe it was the fact that they met in the winter, or maybe it was that fresh snow meant a fresh start for he and Jenn. Whatever it was, he felt good that the case was over and he would be able to see her soon.

Fresher was back in his office just after noon looking over the messages that Samid gave him. There were two that suggested new clients and one that was a follow-up on something he worked on three months earlier. Nothing looked urgent so he picked up the phone and called Jenn Gallager. He reached her voice mail and told her the case was over and he would like to treat her to dinner that night. If he didn't hear back, he would meet her at Glitters on Upper Gage at six o'clock.

As soon as he hung up the phone, Masters entered his office. He couldn't help but notice that she was dressed impeccably, her hair was now lighter blond covering the grey and the small abrasion from Thomas was healed and covered with makeup. He also noticed that her jewelry was colour coordinated with her stunning red dress under her coat.

"Thanks for coming in Mrs. Masters. Let me take your coat. Would you like some coffee?"

Without and taking off her coat or sitting, she replied, "Do you have something to tell me after your trip to Halifax?"

Fresher saw that Masters had returned to her old self. "Yes, I do. Please, have a seat."

Masters sat down but left her coat on. Over the next twenty minutes, Fresher did all the talking and Masters sat listening intently with her face frozen. He gave her all the details, leaving out Miss Jamison's name as he had promised. Fresher could see Masters was comprehending what he was saying but could tell that her mind was drifting off. Oddly, there was no expression on her face given that she had the truth about her brother and the legitimacy of the Trust. Unlike so many other clients, she asked no questions.

"Well Dr. Fresher, I must thank you for your hard work. I also feel badly that you had to deal with Nate Thomas. If I owe any additional money, please send me your bill. If not, keep the remainder."

With that, Rosetta Masters quickly shook Fresher's hand and left the office.

As soon as Masters was out the front door, Samid came into his office.

"Congratulations Harold. You wrapped that up in record time."

"Samid, I wish I felt as good as you do about this. Something is not sitting well with me and I'm not sure what it is. I have never had a client so stiff. I still feel that there are too many things that Masters isn't telling me. I'll figure it out eventually. By the way, finish up the accounting on the case and bill her if it is above the retainer which I suspect it will be given the additional costs of the Wowchuks."

"Will do, and Harold, while you were in with Mrs. Masters, Detective Stiles called and wants to speak with you."

Fresher was exhausted and thought that Stiles wanted to update him on Thomas. He sat back in his chair and called Glitter to make reservations for dinner before he returned Stiles' call.

"Hi Bill, you wanted me to call?"

"Yes Harold. I thought you might be interested in how the Thomas problem finished up."

"Yes, I would. It's still a mystery."

Over the next few minutes, Stiles told Fresher that Thomas was being held without bail and would be charged with assault. They had enough evidence, especially the street sweeper picking Thomas out of a lineup. The Americans had been informed and would not proceed with extradition for the parole violation and Canadian charges could proceed. Stiles best guess was that he would get five years as he had an extensive record.

"Well Bill, I'm glad that he is back where he belongs. Thanks for the update. Take care; I'll talk to you soon."

"Harold, Harold, hold on. There is something else."

"What Bill?"

"I had a chance to talk to Thomas in our jail and asked him why he was after Rosetta Masters. You know what he said? He looked at me with a fierce stare and said, 'Parsons set me up and Rosie knows. I'm gonna get him.' I reminded him Parsons was dead and he just looked at me and gave me a smirk and said, 'I don't think so'."

Those words echoed in Fresher's head. 'I don't think so, I don't think so, I don't think so'.

Bill, do you still have the case file?"

"Yes, why?"

"You told me what happened to Thomas. What happened to Parsons?"

"It says he was killed in prison."

"That's all?"

"Yes."

****

Fresher was at Glitters restaurant fifteen minutes early and was sipping on a tasty Merlot when Jenn walked in. He rose from his chair anticipating a quick hug. Instead, Jenn walked into his arms and accompanied her embrace with a soft kiss on his cheek.

Over dinner, they agreed to see a new theatre production called Annie in Toronto. The play was on stage in the coming summer. They both thought that it would be fun to have a formal evening including dinner at an upscale restaurant.

As dinner was wrapping up, Jenn reached over to Fresher and put her hand on his.

"Harold, you seem a bit distracted tonight. I thought the case was wrapped up?"

"I'm sorry Jenn, I didn't mean to be a wet blanket but you are right. There are a few things about this last case that don't make sense; there are still questions."

"Harold, if your client is happy with the outcome, why aren't you?"

"I guess it's my nature Jenn. It's almost as if I only got part of the story and I don't like that. Unanswered questions give me a certain feeling of not closing a case. On top of that, I received some information after my client left my office that was a bit of a shock."

"Does that mean that the case isn't over?"

"Well, the least I can do is to tell her what I heard and let her make the decision."

Smiling, Jenn quipped. "I'm sure happy I don't have any secrets with you around."

They spent a few minutes talking about the coming weekend. Fresher was hoping to catch up on some rest and Gallager was off to a retreat for the women of the Church.

Outside the restaurant, Fresher walked Gallager to her car. Before opening the door, they embraced and she kissed Fresher's on the cheek. This time he responded.

Once in her car, she rolled down the window and stared up at Fresher with a serious look on her face.

"Harold, I've had people ask me if we're a couple. What should I tell them?"

"Tell them the truth."

"That doesn't help."

Fresher didn't hesitate. "I'd like it to be."

"So would I."

Gallager smiled at Fresher, rolled up the window and pulled out of the parking lot giving two short toots on her horn.

Chapter 8

Fresher couldn't remember when he had an entire weekend to himself and he was going to make the best of it. Relating to Masters what he heard from Stiles could wait until Monday.

After a leisurely breakfast reading the paper from cover to cover, he visited a car dealer. His eight year old sedan was beginning to show signs of needing repair and in the back of his mind, he thought that it would be nice if he had something newer and more comfortable if he and Jenn were going to be seeing each other more. Relaxing in his favourite chair glancing over the automotive brochures and looking forward to a simple night of pizza and watching a movie, the Masters case found its way back into his head. He couldn't get Thomas' comments out of his mind, 'Parsons set me up and Rosie knows. I'm gonna get him'.

The rest of the weekend, other things came back to him. Masters said she didn't know Thomas until it was forced out of her; the way she dismissed Fresher when he last met with her; the question of how a biker bunny turned bookkeeper wound up living a caviar lifestyle. Too many questions remained.

Monday morning, he arrived at the office the same time as Samid. Over a cup of coffee together, they exchanged weekend activities.

"Harold, my brother said he saw you having dinner with a woman. Can I assume it's Jenn Gallager, the woman that has left messages for you in the past few months?"

"Yes, you can assume that." Fresher wanted to change the subject.

"Samid, I am not sure that the Masters case is closed. I need you to do two things for me. First, look into the death of a Joey Parsons. According to reports, he was killed in a knife fight the first day in prison. She says she read about it just after New Years so it would have been late December 1976. Second, can you call Masters and see if she can come in today after work. I have information for her and it's not something that I want to do over the phone.

Just after lunch, Samid came into Fresher's office with papers in his hand.

"Harold, I spent most of the morning on the phone with the archivist at the Calgary newspaper. It took her some time but she found two articles and faxed me copies."

Fresher took the papers and read them. The first article was short and reported that Joey Parsons was killed in the Alberta Institution. The second article, two days later was more detailed. It reported that Joey Parsons, recently convicted of several offences, was stabbed in a prison fight. Mr. Parsons was taken to the prison infirmary, then transferred to an ambulance where he died on route to hospital. There was no next of kin and the province buried Mr. Parsons.

Mrs. Masters arrived at four forty five. Fresher's eyebrows lifted a bit as she walked in wearing in a yellow pantsuit and again with matching jewelry. As usual, the hair and makeup were impeccable. She looked annoyed to having been called and stood waiting for Fresher to say something.

"Thank you for coming by. Would you like a coffee?"

She ignored Fresher's question. "I thought the mystery of the money was solved. Will this take long?"

"Mrs. Masters, please have a seat. I have some information that came to me after we last met and I think you should know."

"Dr. Fresher, you said that you proved that Bruno's money was made legally and Thomas is back in jail. What else do I need to know?"

Fresher couldn't believe how curt Masters was. He was expecting some attitude, but this was beyond the woman he knew during the past couple of weeks.

"Mrs. Masters, it deals with comments made by Nate Thomas after his arrest that raise questions, comments that have a direct impact on you."

"I seriously doubt that he would have anything to say that, as you put it, 'have direct impact me,'" she said almost sarcastically.

Both Masters and Fresher were silent for several seconds until Masters sat down and asked Fresher what he was talking about.

"Mrs. Masters, Thomas was interrogated by the police after his arrest. I will be exact as to what he said. 'Parsons set me up and Rosie knows. I'm gonna get him.'

Masters stared at Fresher. The scowl on her face disappeared and she unconsciously slowly shook her head from side to side.

"Are you saying that Joey is still alive?"

"I don't know but Thomas thinks so, and he seems to think you know where he is. That is why he came after you."

"Joey isn't alive, he couldn't be." Fresher saw her entire demeanor then change. "Are you sure?"

"I am not sure of anything. I was able to get copies of the newspaper articles that say he was killed, but how do you discount what Thomas said."

Masters slunk back in the chair staring at Fresher. "What can we do?"

"Mrs. Masters, this isn't a 'we' problem. I am just delivering a message that I thought you would be interested in. My work on your case is finished."

Masters got up from the chair and slowly walked to the door. She stopped and turned.

"Harold, would you be interested in looking into this for me?"

Fresher's head went back slightly. He knew that she was shaken.

"I assume you want me to see if Joey Parsons is still alive."

"Yes, but I can't believe it. I read it in the newspaper and I got a package from the Dark Destiny three days after the article.

"A package?"

"Yes, money, a lot of money in the envelope with a printed note that said 'they were sorry Joey died and to use the money to go find a life'."

"Money?"

"Yes, over $50,000. They wouldn't lie to me."

"Was the note signed?"

"No, as I said, and the bottom had DD, the gang's logo."

"Did the other girls get the same?"

"I don't know. As I told you, the girls were gone before the trials were over."

"So you never kept in contact with them?"

"No."

"Mrs. Masters, I need to ask you something that may be none of my business. Is that the money that allows you to live what I see as an expensive life style?"

"Yes and there is more. When I arrived in Hamilton, I overheard people at work talking about buying rental properties and I needed to do something with the money so I bought three small houses on Hamilton beach. I sold two over the years for a substantial profit."

"And you work?"

"I job share two days a week. It keeps me busy. Harold, will you help me now?"

Fresher knew she was reaching out. It was the second time she called him 'Harold'. He took a half minute to mull her request over in his mind.

"Mrs. Masters, I will see what I can do but I can tell you right now that getting any information from Thomas will be almost impossible to obtain since he is in jail and the police don't usually lie about a prisoner killed in jail. I'll need a retainer that you can drop off with Samid on the way out. Also one more thing, do you have a picture of Parsons?"

"Yes, I have a quite a few and will drop some off tomorrow morning."

Fresher watched as Masters put on her coat and leave without saying another word. As soon as he heard the front door close, he called Samid into his office.

"Harold, Masters gave me another cheque, this time for $5,000. I am assuming that there is a second case."

"Yes, there is but I am not sure that I can get the answers that Mrs. Masters is looking for. Thomas said Joey Parsons is still alive."

"Really?"

"Yes."

"Where are you going to start?"

"I have a few ideas. I need you to look into her background from the day she came to Hamilton. She said she arrived in January 1977 just after she lost her baby. That's when she changed her name from Riso to Masters. I don't know when she started working at the steel company but she told me a few days ago that she studied bookkeeping while she was in Calgary. Whatever you do, be discrete.

"Harold, I am sensing that you think that Mrs. Masters still hasn't told you the whole story."

"You have that right Samid. I am going to give her a day to let Thomas' comments sink in before I try to get more information from her."

The next morning, Samid found an envelope in the mailbox as he was unlocking the door. When Fresher came in, four pictures of Joey Parsons lay on his desk. Three of the pictures included Masters and two more people. Parsons was at least two inches taller than the other men in the photos. The fourth picture was Parsons leaning up against his motorcycle. He had striking features set off by short brown hair and brown eyes. He was clean shaven and he smiled with both his eyes and his mouth. Although the picture was several years old, Fresher knew that those features would remain with him until he died.

Fresher made a call to Stiles.

"Hi Bill."

"Hi Harold. I guess your client is safe and happy with Thomas out of the way."

"Yes, she feels better, but there is something that is bothering me Bill. Why would Thomas be so adamant that Parsons is still alive? How did you read him when he said that?"

"To tell you the truth, I believed him. He had nothing to gain or lose by saying that, and frankly I doubt he would risk going back to jail for a 'feeling'."

"That is interesting. When I told her what Thomas said, I got a strong feeling that she was shocked but wasn't sure to believe Thomas or not."

"Two people, two stories. Nothing unusual about that."

"Bill, you told me that there were a couple of pages missing from the file. Is there any way they were misfiled?"

"No, I checked more than once."

"Can you do me and……"

"Harold, before you ask, I can't send or fax you a copy. It isn't a simple break and enter; it's involves international drugs and murder."

"Well, can you pull your copy and give me a verbal summary of the page before the missing pages?"

"Sure, give me a few minutes."

Stiles came back to the phone and Fresher could hear him leafing through the file.

"Here it is. Let's see. Yes, the page deals with court sentencing. Thomas, Bowen and Parsons were shipped off to Federal Penitentiary, Thomas and Bowen to BC and Parsons to the Alberta Institution in Saskatchewan. The last entry is the transfer of Parsons from the local jail to prison. As I told you, there are also newspaper clippings describing Parsons' knifing."

"Harold, why the interest in this? I thought you finished the case?"

"I finished the first case. Now she has asked me to see if there is any truth to Parsons being alive. Perhaps Thomas can help."

"Good luck with that Harold. Thomas is being held in isolation until the Crown is ready start proceedings. You can't get to him."

"Who is his lawyer?"

"Just a public defender."

"Can I talk to him?"

"What do you need to know? He'll probably let me know before a person not in the police department."

"Simple Bill. Why does he feel he was set up and why does he think Parsons is alive?"

"I'll see what I can do."

****

Late that afternoon, Samid hurried into Fresher's office with a big smile on his face, clutching a piece of paper.

"Harold, you won't believe what I found."

"Right now, I wouldn't be surprised if Masters was really married with ten children."

"You're close."

Fresher jerked upright in his chair. "I don't understand."

"Rosetta Masters had a son. There may have been an accident in Calgary, but the child didn't die."

"Why doesn't this information surprise me?"

Samid laid out the entire story. With the information that Fresher gave him, he checked the Hamilton birth registry starting May 1977. There was nothing as far out as October, so I looked at the registry for Toronto. There it was. In late July, Joseph Masters was born to mother Rosetta Masters. There was no father's name registered.

"Well done Samid, well done."

Chapter 9

Fresher called Masters and asked her if he could drop by her condo for a few minutes. He needed some information that would help him in his search for Joey assuming he was alive. She didn't hestitate.

As Fresher drove up, he was again impressed with the grandeur of the building. His thoughts went to Jenn imagining them being together and living here. His imagination passed quickly as he approached Masters' unit.

Rosetta Masters answered the door wearing a very elaborate outfit, a style he only saw in magazines and her scent was not the typical Avon. "Dr. Fresher, please come in and have a seat. Can I get you anything?"

"No thank you."

"What information do you need?"

Fresher was prepared for this moment and he had to make sure that the he didn't leave until he got what he needed or he was prepared to give her back the retainer and drop the case.

"Mrs. Masters, I am going to be very blunt with you. You have kept information back and even lied to me. It's hard enough for me to get answers without you putting up roadblocks."

Masters sat stunned and Fresher didn't let her speak.

"You told me you didn't recognize Thomas' picture and you left out a lot of your Calgary life. Now I find out that you have a son."

The room went silent.

Almost whispering, she asked, "How did you find out?"

"That doesn't matter. What matters is that if I can find out, anyone else could. Why didn't you tell me?"

"You don't understand biker families. I was afraid that with Joey gone, my child and I would be 'inherited' by one of the guys. No one knew I was pregnant and once I got the money and the go ahead to leave, I was gone hoping that no one would find out."

"So the only person that knew was your brother and that's why he changed the Trust to 'And Family'."

"Yes. I should also tell you that the reason I didn't go to the funeral is that my son was in the hospital with a throat infection. I needed to stay with him."

"Where is the boy?"

Masters was fidgeting and as soon as she was about to speak, her mouth closed.

"Look Mrs. Masters, this case has been tough enough. I need as much information as possible and right now you are the only source I have."

"He is finishing his last year of high school as a resident student at St. Andrews College in Aurora Ontario. He's been there for his entire schooling and is doing so well, both his grades and his athletics. I only see him every month or so. Even in the summer, he stays and works at a nearby farm.

That is a picture of him on the table in the corner. I took it last summer." Her eyes widened and her voice got louder. "Do you think he is safe?"

"Yes, he is safe. If Thomas knew, he would have used the boy to get to you. I need to know your entire story, all of it."

Masters got up, poured a glass of wine, sat down, and took a long sip before she started. While she was up, Fresher looked closer at the boy's picture and could see the strong resemblance to Parsons.

Masters sat back down and started. Everything she told Fresher so far was true. She knew that Joey was on the wrong side of law and soon found out that the Skeletons were an elite part of Dark Destiny. She feared that it was only a matter of time before something bad would happen and it did.

"Mrs. Masters, what was Joey like? According to the timeline, you lived with him for over two years. Surely you got to know him fairly well."

"Harold, I saw a side of Joey that he kept very secret."

Fresher heard 'Harold' and saw that different person, one that was again less abrasive and abrupt.

"What do you mean 'a side of Joey'?"

"Where do I start?"

"His habits, the good side, the bad side, things that made him different from the others."

"Well, I can tell you that he wasn't like a couple of the others in the house. He seldom had more than two drinks and never touched drugs. I can recall many nights when the other three men would get so drunk that they fought and even beat their girls. They were all into drugs, but Wally Bowen was into it big time, and never had a girl because of that. A lot of money went down the drain because of the booze and drugs."

"Was there a lot of money involved?"

"I never knew for sure. I know that the other girls had trouble getting cash for new clothes or makeup. Nate gave Jill an allowance but she always complained it was childish and wasn't enough. I think Mandy got a bit more, but not much. In my case, Joey never refused me money for what I needed. I think that was one of the reasons I stayed with him. He treated me like someone special."

"Mrs. Masters, was there anything that you can recall between Joey and Thomas?"

"He and Joey were always a bit edgy with each other, but nothing violent. I knew that Thomas used drugs. Perhaps that had something to do with it."

"But you told me before that he forgot his medication when he left. Are you sure it wasn't drugs?"

"Absolutely not. As I told you, he was having trouble with his muscles. Sometimes during the night, he would walk up telling me his arm or leg was numb and once I saw him stumble getting in the car. It was as if he lost his balance."

"So no bad habits for Joey except being on the wrong side of the law?"

"He had a very quick temper, but only for the right reasons. He didn't take any crap from anyone including the other men in the gang. I remember once when a member named Max Rosen made a play on me during a party at the big clubhouse, Joey pinned him up against the wall and threatened him with a knife. That was the only time that any of the men came near me. I also saw him bring the guys in line when we were out for the night having dinner somewhere. He didn't tolerate any abuse directed at waitresses or others in the restaurant. I even recall him stepping in between a married couple fighting in a parking lot. Go figure, a patched motorcycle gang member playing mediator"

"It sounds like he really liked you."

"Yes, and I loved him. There was no doubt in my mind. We began sleeping together after two months and as far as I knew, it was a monogamous relationship. The only thing that I didn't like was that he always slept with a hand gun under his pillow."

"Mrs. Masters, you mentioned a few days ago that Mandy took off as soon as she heard Marcel Orte was killed during the ambush by the agents. You also said that Jill left the house the day after Nate was convicted. Did you know where she went?"

"No. I remember her telling me that she was from Brandon but it wouldn't surprise me if she went to BC and waited for Nate to be released."

"Why would you say that?"

"Jill was very insecure and Nate was her lifeline."

"But you told me that she received an allowance and thought he was treating her like a child."

"Harold, you need to understand that many of the girls came from an abusive environment and once they found a man that provided any kind of safety and security, they were committed."

"What is Jill's last name?"

"Coy."

"Is there anything else?"

"Something did happen that I recently thought may have something to do with Thomas finding me. About two years after I came east, I bumped into Jill Coy in Toronto at the bus station. I was standing in the lineup going back to Hamilton and I heard 'Rosie'. I turned and there was a woman looking at me saying, 'Rosie Riso". In a reflex action, I said, no it's Masters. Then I realized that it was Jill. The exchange was brief. She told me she was now living in Vancouver, but in Toronto for her mother's funeral. That was it. Frankly, we both had too much bad history to extend our discussion."

"Let's get back to Joey. Anything that was really unique?"

"Yes, and it was very personal and private to Joey. Once it became serious between us, he asked me to take a trip one Saturday. We took the car and drove to one of a dozen ranches outside of Calgary. Although each man had a motorcycle, they shared two cars. Joey always liked to take the roomy Lincoln. Once at the farm, he would rent two horses for a couple of hours and we would go horseback riding."

"Horseback riding?"

"Yes, regardless of the weather, summer and winter. He so loved to ride. He was always gentle with the horse; it was as if he knew exactly what to do to have them respond. In the good weather, we would find a quiet place and just lay on the grass enjoying the day."

"Mrs. Masters, I know you loved him, but are you being a bit too complimentary about a biker?"

"No Harold. That was Joey."

"Did Joey have any personal habits?"

"Not sure if this is what you are looking for but he always said 'merci' instead of thanks. It became a trademark. It didn't matter where he was or who he was with."

"Did he speak French?"

"He never spoke French to me, but there was something that I couldn't understand. Every time we went to the ranches, he stopped at a convenience store not too far from the house to pick up some snacks. I never went in but could see through the window that the clerk was a very tall, attractive blond. More than once I thought that he went there just to see her so I made up an excuse to inside. I was going to ask him not to forget some diet pop. When I went into the store, he was talking to her. I couldn't hear the discussion until I got closer. I thought it was French. They saw me and continued in English. Back in the car he sensed I was jealous and put his arm around me and told me not to worry; he was mine. He was so sweet."

"What can you tell me about Joey's background?"

"How far back do you want to go?"

"As far as you know."

Masters reminded Fresher that Joey was orphaned when he was young and bounced around foster homes for half a dozen years. He spent the rest of his teens and early twenties either behind bars, unemployed or being a construction labourer. Eventually, he made enough money to buy a bike and became an independent rider until he joined up with the Dark Destiny. The Skeletons were created two years later. Strangely, Joey told her that he wasn't in favour of the skeleton tattoos, but went along. His tattoo was on his upper left forearm. Masters put her head down for a few seconds and with a tear in her eye, told Fresher that a couple of days before the arrests, he came back from a meeting in Calgary, he was quiet and after a late dinner, they went to their room. Joey reached for her and they made love as if it was their first time only he didn't wear a condom. He told her that he loved her more than once. She believed that it was the night she conceived.

"Mrs. Masters, did you keep any mementos of the time you spent together with Joey?"

"I think a son is the best memento I could possibly have."

Fresher looked at Masters sympathetically and paused before he continued. "Assuming that Joey is still alive and I find him, should he know about his son?"

"No, I would prefer to do that."

Fresher left Masters condominium with a completely different opinion of her and with a few pieces of information that he could work with.

Chapter 10

The next morning, Fresher was in his office on the phone with a man trying to convince him that he didn't take on cases that involve lost animals. He appreciated that the cat was an important part of the family, but the best solution for the man was to post pictures on poles and offer a reward. Samid came in just as Fresher was hanging up the telephone.

"Harold, I was looking over your notes from yesterday's meeting with Rosetta Masters. You wrote that Parsons was on medication and later in the report you jotted down, 'numbness and loss of balance'."

"Yes. I thought originally that the medication bottle was disguising hard drugs, but the muscle twitching was real according to Masters."

"Harold, what she described could have been MS."

"Multiple Sclerosis?"

"Sounds like it. I went to college with a girl with MS and those were the symptoms."

Samid went back to his desk leaving Fresher with a possible new twist to the mystery but not long to think about it as his phone rang.

"Good morning Harold."

"Hello Bill. I assume that you couldn't get the public defender to get any information from Thomas."

"On the contrary, and you better sit down. If Thomas is telling the truth, you have a real mystery on your hands."

Stiles went on to tell Fresher the public defender suggested he could make a deal for Thomas with the prosecution but needed the entire Parsons' story. To the public defender's surprise, Thomas opened up. Once he was convicted in 1976, the gang cut him loose making the first few months in prison very hard time before he was suddenly reinstated and served the remainder of his time back under the strength of the club. He didn't know why the club abandoned him for those first few months until four years later when another Dark Destiny was sent to the same prison for attempted murder. Thomas was told that the ambush in 1976 was the result of an informer, and the club originally thought it was Thomas but now knew it wasn't him, as any informer would have gone into protective custody and eventually disappear.

"Harold, it's the next piece of information that you are after. After Thomas served fourteen years in Canada, he was in a holding tank waiting for transport to the USA. There were three others with him. One was from Alberta Institution and when Thomas asked him if knew a biker by the name 'Parsons', the guy just laughed at him and told him that he was in the infirmary the day Parsons was knifed and from his standpoint, the injury wasn't close to being fatal. An ambulance picked up Parsons and the next thing the guy heard was a report of Parsons' death. It was at that point that Thomas suspected Parsons was the informer and cost Thomas and Wally Bowen fourteen years of their life. Thomas told the public defender that he spent the next two years planning and thought that Masters was his best starting point. Jill had already mentioned seeing Masters in Toronto heading to Hamilton and saw the name on her bag, 'Masters'. The rest is obvious."

At 8:30 a.m. sharp, Fresher called Marsha Milligan.

"Good morning Marsha, it's Harold Fresher"

"Harold. Good to hear from you. Need more information about the Trust?"

"No, it turns out that all is well."

"So what can I do for you?"

"You mentioned that you attended some legal conferences over the years. I was wondering if you recall any of the Crown staff in Alberta."

"I keep all the business cards. Hold on, let me check. Yes. A few years ago, I met Stewart Hoskins. His card says he is the Assistant Crown Attorney for the province of Alberta."

Fresher took the contact information for Hoskins, thanked Milligan and hung up. He busied himself with a new file until it was just after 8:00 a.m. in the morning in Edmonton and he took a chance that Hoskins was still on staff and would be in the office. The phone rang three times before it was answered.

"Good morning, Alberta Attorney General's Office. How may I direct your call?"

"Stewart Hoskins, please."

"One moment please."

Fresher was happy to know that Hoskins was still on the job and waited anxiously until he reached Hoskins' voice mail. He left a message for Hoskins to call stressing his title, Doctor hoping that this would compel Hoskins to call back soon.

It was late mid afternoon when his phone rang.

"Dr. Fresher, may I help you?"

"Hello Dr. Fresher. This is Stewart Hoskins, Assistant Crown Attorney in Alberta. You left me a message."

"Yes. Thank you for returning my call. I am a private investigator in Hamilton and....." Hoskins cut him off.

"Dr. Fresher, Harold Fresher? You probably don't remember me. We were in the same class for one semester in Toronto in 1962 before I transferred to Manitoba University."

Fresher had a very vague recollection of Hoskins. "Oh, yes, I recall Stewart. You had a car accident just before Christmas and transferred to Man U because they had better handicap facilities. It's great to reconnect. How are you doing?"

"Still using two canes Harold, but all in all, things have gone very well. In fact, I was so inspired by that one semester, I not only finished my post grad in criminology, I went on to my law degree. How about you? I heard you are at RMC."

"Was at RMC. I now have my own investigation firm in Hamilton."

"How is that going?"

"Excellent."

"That's great. So, what can I do for you Harold?"

"Stewart. Listen, I have an unusual case that involves the Dark Destiny, a motorcycle gang in Alberta."

"I heard of them. Not sure if they are still around. Is this about a something that happened recently?"

"No, it goes back a few years. A few of the gang were arrested in 1976. It seems that they were drug trafficking across the border and a combined USA-Canada task force took them down. I am trying to get information on one of the members. His name is Joey Parsons and the only information I have is that he was sentenced to fourteen years in the Alberta Institute in late November 1976 but was killed in a knife fight the first day in prison. The file I was able to access through the local police was missing some detail near the beginning, but I learned that after he was stabbed he died on the way to the hospital. I saw an old newspaper clipping about his death."

There was a long pause at the other end of the phone.

"Harold, if this Parsons guy is dead, wouldn't he be in a cemetery?"

"That's where things get a bit confusing. I have it from a source that Parsons could be alive and may even have tipped off the authorities before the task force moved in."

There was another long pause before Hoskins spoke. "Harold, why are you looking for Joey Parsons?"

Fresher was reluctant to involve Masters or Thomas in the discussion so he deflected. "It's complicated suffice to say that an old friend of Parsons is involved. Look Stewart, I don't want you to get into any trouble but any information would be useful."

"Well, there isn't much to go on. Harold, give me a day or so and I'll see what I can do."

Fresher sat in his office for the rest of the afternoon adding comments to a report for Masters. As he finished, he decided to call Jenn and see how her weekend went at the retreat. He reached for the phone, but it rang before he could pick up the receiver. It was Hoskins.

"Harold, its Stewart Hoskins."

"Thanks for calling Stewart."

"I found the report, but it doesn't tell me much more than what you said regarding Parsons being stabbed in the mess hall and taken to the infirmary. He died in the ambulance on his way to the nearby hospital. His body was transported to the city morgue. That's it."

"Stewart, I understand that Parsons was buried by the Province. Is that normal?"

"Yes, it would be if no one came forward to claim the body. Hold on for a minute."

Hoskins came back to the phone and told Fresher that on the original arrest report, Parsons declared that he had no next of kin.

"I wonder why Dark Destiny didn't come forward. That is strange."

"Maybe not. After the killings and arrests, Dark Destiny went to war with the mob, both blaming each other for the ambush. Burying Parsons would be the last thing they had time for."

"Stewart, where would Parsons be buried?"

"A supplementary report says Parsons is in a pauper's grave near Saskatoon. That would have been the closest site to the hospital where his body was taken. Those cemeteries don't have visible markers, just numbers. You would need to access the city files and I can tell you that they wouldn't give information to you without a judge's order. Unless your client is a relative, it just won't happen"

"It looks like I have run out of ways to find Joey Parsons. Is there a file on the lead-up to the ambush and arrests, perhaps something that explains the ambush?"

"Harold, that information is way above my pay grade. Even if I could get it access to it, the information would be over fifteen years old and probably useless."

"Stewart, I can't thank you enough. It was great to reconnect."

"You're welcome Harold. Hope it all works out for your client."

Fresher couldn't go back to Masters with anything unproven, especially some unsubstantiated information from Nate Thomas. It would only get her hopes up and if his suspicions were wrong, she would be devastated.

That evening, Fresher stayed in the office going over all of the Masters file notes and organizing the final report.

It was just after 9:00 p.m. when the phone rang. Odd, he thought, it must be a wrong number.

"Dr. Fresher, may I help you?"

"Hello Harold. I thought I would get your voice mail."

"Stewart? Are you working late?"

"No, I'm at home. Speaking of working late, how come you are still in the office?"

"Actually, I'm finishing up some paperwork. So, to what do I owe this call?"

"Do you remember Michael Bouleau?"

"Michael Bouleau?" No, the name doesn't ring a bell."

"Sure you do. He sat beside us at school in Toronto. We even had a few beers with him after study hall."

"Stewart, I honestly don't recognize the name."

"Harold, he was the guy that wanted to work for the RCMP and used to bore us with his aspirations to catching bad guys. Give it time, you'll remember him."

After a few more exchanges between the two men, Hoskins hung up. Fresher thought that Hoskins probably had a few drinks and was reminiscing about his college days and got things mixed up.

It wasn't two minutes later than Fresher connected the dots. The file leading up to the arrest was sealed but Hoskins must have read it over. Was Joey Parsons really Michael Bouleau? The reference to 'working for the RCMP and having aspirations to catching bad guys' couldn't be a random comment. Had Hoskins just unlocked the door for his old school chum?

Fresher didn't sleep well that night and was in the office shortly after seven thirty in the morning. His entire focus that day would be finding Michael Bouleau and the first thing he needed to do was to call Rosetta Masters and confirm some key details. As he was about to call Masters, Samid came in.

"Harold, this makes twice this week that you made the morning coffee. Couldn't sleep?"

"Not much last night because there may be a case breaker."

Fresher went on to tell Samid about the call from Hoskins and the probability that Joey Parsons could really be Michael Bouleau. Now there was a much bigger question - was Bouleau working undercover for the government and his death arranged to get him free? Fresher asked Samid to begin a nationwide search for Michael Bouleau. He reminded Samid about the love for horses and the possibility he spoke French.

Rejuvenated with a new lead, Fresher made a phone call. "Good morning Mrs. Masters. Sorry to call so early but I wanted to talk about a few specific things about Joey."

Over the next fifteen minutes, Fresher needed to confirm certain things that Masters told him. Specifically, she never spoke to Joey after he left the day he was arrested, the money came after Joey was shot, he always stopped at the same convenience store on the way to a ranch, she heard him speaking French to the clerk, and she was sure he ignored her during the trial and didn't know she was pregnant.

"Harold, do you think that Joey is still alive?"

Fresher heard the hope in her voice. "Mrs. Masters, to be very honest with you, I am not still sure but I intend to know in the next couple of days. Please don't get your hopes up. Remember, this notion of him being alive came from Nate Thomas and I don't trust him."

Fresher spent the rest of the morning in the library with Samid leafing through telephone directories. By noon, they finished British Columbia and Saskatchewan feeing that it would be improbable that if Parsons was alive, he wouldn't be in Alberta.

"Samid, if Bouleau spoke French, let's concentrate on Quebec and New Brunswick. We can always do the other provinces if we strike out.

It was mid afternoon when Samid tapped Fresher on the shoulder.

"Have a look at this. White Birch Ranch in Woodstock New Brunswick. Do you know what 'Birch' is in French? Bouleau. There is a yellow pages advertisement. The ranch caters to children and adults with disabilities and it says, 'Ask for Corri or Michael'."

"Well done Samid. This can't be a coincidence. I'm going to grab the first available flight to Fredericton."

Chapter 11

The ninety minute drive in his rental car was time to reinforce his thinking that there was a tie between Bouleau and White Birch Ranch. It certainly was a unique approach, tying his name with his business. Fresher recalled that the Ranch advertised specializing in people with disabilities. That was another uniqueness about the business. Bouleau no doubt thought it through. The ranch was close to the US border, which would be good for business.

Fresher was quite impressed as he approached the Ranch; he could tell that the place was well maintained. A white perimeter fence stretched as far as he could see on both sides of a gated laneway. The spring grass on the outside was beginning to green up and several horses of various colours grazed inside the fence. Fresher stopped in front of a wide ornate iron gate and saw a call box on the left gatepost. He rolled down the window and pushed the button. Within a few seconds, a woman's voice came through the speaker.

"May I help you?"

"My name is Doctor Harold Fresher and I would like to see Michael Bouleau." He waited several seconds before a response.

"Do you have an appointment?"

"No I don't, but this is important."

"Once the gate is open Doctor, drive to the main house. I'll meet you there."

Fresher waited for the gate to open then drove a quarter of a mile on a smooth gravel road to a large single story ranch style house sitting in front of two horse barns in the rear. The sides of the barns were dotted with smaller fence enclosures containing smaller horses at the water trough or hay piles. It was all very impressive. As Fresher exited the car, a tall blond very fit woman in jeans and a shirt smiled at him and approached with her hand outstretched. As she got closer, he saw an extremely beautiful woman in her mid fifties and he could tell that her beauty was natural. Fresher's thoughts went back to how Masters described the tall, attractive blond in the convenience store. Could this be the same woman?

"Dr. Fresher, my name is Corri Birch. How can I help you?"

"I would like to speak with Michael Bouleau. It's a personal matter."

"Doctor, does this have to do with one of your patients?"

"Not exactly but I do have a client that he will want to learn about."

Fresher could sense that she wasn't sure if she should retrieve Michael or not. Finally, she said, "Come in and have a seat. I will get him.

Fresher followed her in to a large room with wooden floors, wooden walls and a peaked wooded ceiling. There was a large stone fireplace on one wall and various western theme art pieces on the others. The furniture was dark brown leather. The room could have been a movie set for a western.

A few minutes later, Fresher heard a man call his name. When he turned around, it was no mistaking Joey Parsons. The photo of a much younger Parsons confirmed this. He also noticed the lower half of a black tattoo of a skeleton's hand below a rolled up sleeve on his arm. Bouleau was sitting in a wheelchair.

"Dr. Fresher, my sister tells me that you are here for one of your patients."

'Sister?' That was a surprise', he thought, different last names.

Fresher started by handing Bouleau a business card and telling him that he was a private investigator from Hamilton and everything that they would talk about would be confidential.

"Mr. Bouleau I think you need to listen to a story."

"Dr. Fresher, before you start, let's have a coffee and chat." Bouleau handed the business card to his sister. She got up and went to another room.

While his sister was gone the get coffee, Bouleau explained the workings of the ranch and the value it has brought to so many handicapped adults and children. This was a busy time of year as it was well into April and they were within a few weeks of opening for the season. His own situation, having multiple sclerosis, required him to use forearm crutches or a wheelchair. He acknowledged true appreciation of the value of how horses delivered an opportunity to make challenged people feel connected and special.

'Multiple sclerosis', another indicator this was Joey Parsons.

Ten minutes later, Birch came back in to the room, nodded yes to her brother, and handed the business card back to him.

With a smile on his face, Bouleau casually asked, "So what is this about?"

"I was hired to see if you have a past, a past that included a man named Joey Parsons."

Still smiling, Bouleau responded, "Well, well. My past has finally caught up to me."

Surprised at Bouleau's candor, Fresher simply said, 'yes'.

"Dr. Fresher, you said that this discussion was confidential."

"Yes. The courts recognize that investigator-client information is privileged."

"Why don't you tell me what you know before I answer any questions?"

The request to tell all was not Fresher's usual way of doing business, but since Bouleau was so honest, he complied and began by relating Nate Thomas threatening Rosetta Masters, known to Bouleau as Rose Riso. He fast forwarded the discussion to Thomas making a statement that Bouleau was still alive and Thomas was after him.

Bouleau snickered. "Nate Thomas. Now that's a name we haven't heard for several years. Well, it doesn't surprise us that he thought I was alive. It's impossible to keep some secrets."

Fresher was miffed that Bouleau was so nonchalant about learning that Thomas was after him and it was an, 'us' issue. He also noticed that Birch was sitting relaxed with a slight grin on her face.

"You're right. I found you so I guess others could and that is where Rose Riso comes in."

Bouleau turned his head and looked at his sister before returning his attention to Fresher. "How is Rosie?"

"Doing very well. She lives in Hamilton and has established a comfortable life, thanks to the envelope of cash you left for her."

Bouleau nodded his head up and down slowly acknowledging what Fresher had just said. "Dr. Fresher, why did she hire you?"

"To be exact, she asked me to 'see if Joey Parsons is alive and what the issue is between the two men'. Mr. Bouleau, why do you think Thomas was so aggressive trying to find you? "

Birch leaned forward in her chair. "Dr. Fresher, the answer to the first question is obvious. You know that the stabbing was a set up. Sure, Michael was cut, but he did that himself with a tin spoon during an altercation Michael started with another inmate. Once he got to the infirmary, the physician was part of the plan to send Michael to the hospital. Federal agents picked him up in the ambulance and released him at the bus station in Saskatoon."

"I am guessing that Thomas was correct in figuring out that you were the informer Michael," Fresher offered.

Bouleau offered, "Yes, you are right. Well it really doesn't matter. He knows. The question is can anyone find me?"

"My guess is no. He assumed Rose would know where you were but she didn't. In addition, he wouldn't have the information I have, the stuff that led to me finding you. Frankly, it may not matter. Thomas was caught a few days ago. There were several charges including assault. He won't be out for a few years."

Birch offered, "And there really isn't any threat from Dark Destiny. Those folks are a thing of the past."

"Dr. Fresher, how did you figure this all out?" Bouleau asked.

"I don't want to appear cocky, but that is what I am paid for."

"But you still needed the connection to the farm and the name change," he continued.

Fresher knew he had to be careful not to mention Stewart Hoskins' involvement. "Rose said you were a horse enthusiast, she heard you speak French and you were on medication that my office concluded were the symptoms of MS. The rest was just a process of elimination looking for anything that combined these factors, but the real clue was connecting the words 'Birch' and 'Bouleau'."

"Well done." Bouleau responded.

"So, what is the whole story?"

During the next half hour, the brother and sister took turns relating how Bouleau was working undercover and the fake death was the perfect plan to disappear. The plan worked for several years.

"Mrs. Birch, you were the one working in the convenience store, weren't you?"

"You're good Dr. Fresher, very good. By the way, it's Ms Birch."

Fresher was now confused but didn't want to change the subject. "Thank you Ms Birch, but if you don't mind, there are a few loose ends that you could help me with, the first being what your involvement was."

"Dr. Fresher', Bouleau broke in, "As I understand your case it was to see if Joey Parsons was still alive and why Thomas was after me. You have done that. I suppose you will go back to Hamilton and report to Rose. What she does with the information is up to her but I ask you to respect the confidentiality of this discussion keeping in mind that my sister and I have been looking behind us for many years."

"You are right. My job was to see if you were still alive and I will report just that, not where you are. In addition, there is no need for her to know that you were an informer. That information could be valuable to others. I will be speaking with her as soon as possible and it is up to you if you want Rose to have details."

Fresher drove away from the ranch not completely satisfied with his findings, but enough to tell Masters that Parsons was still alive but given the nature of the undercover work, he could not expose him.

****

Before boarding the flight back to Toronto, Fresher called Masters.

"Mrs. Masters. I have some news for you."

"Good news?"

"I think you need to decide if it's good news. Joey Parsons is still alive. He has a new name and a new life. I met with him and he has no interest in reconnecting with you due to personal circumstances."

"Did you tell him he had a son?"

"No, you asked me not to so I didn't."

"Did he know why Thomas was after him?"

"No." Fresher could not divulge the probability that Thomas knew Bouleau set up the ambush.

There was a long pause before Masters spoke. "Dr. Fresher, I really want to speak with him."

"I can't give you his contact information. As I said, there are circumstances."

There was another long pause before Masters spoke. "Do you think that he would change his mind if he knew he had a son?"

"Are you asking me to tell him in the hope you would be able to talk to him?"

Masters responded quickly. "Yes, tell him and ask him if we can talk."

It was late afternoon and his flight was due to leave in less than an hour. Realizing that the call to Bouleau could be long, he rescheduled for the last flight out that night before he phoned the ranch.

"Ms Birch, its Dr. Fresher."

"Is this call to tell us that Rose knows where we are?"

"No, I told you that I wouldn't tell her that. Can I speak to your brother? It is extremely important."

"Hold on."

A few minutes passed before Michael Bouleau picked up the receiver."

"Dr. Fresher?"

"Yes."

"What could be so extremely important? Did Thomas escape?"

"Mr. Bouleau, there is only one way to say this; Rose has asked me to tell you that you fathered a son with her."

Fresher could hear Bouleau inhale. "Where are you Dr. Fresher?"

"At the airport."

"Can you come back to the ranch? We shouldn't talk about this over the phone."

Fresher had already returned the rental car and the agent looked confused when he appeared back in front of the counter. Fresher smiled sheepishly as he signed the rental agreement and took possession of the keys.

As he approached the ranch gate, there was no need to push the button; the gates swung open. Fresher hadn't got out of the car when the house door opened and Corri Birch waved him in. Michael Bouleau was sitting in a large wing chair with the wheelchair beside him. No sooner than Fresher sat in a chair facing Michael Bouleau, the questions started.

"You said on the phone that I fathered a son. Why didn't you tell me earlier?"

"I was instructed not to. Rose wanted to do that but you refused to see her and I suspect she asked me to do it so you would agree to meet."

"How can you be sure the boy is mine?"

"I can't be sure without a blood test but Rose's story is credible. The timing is right and she described the night you had unprotected intimacy. She tried to tell you during the trial by sending you a note, but you crumpled the paper without even reading it. He is only sixteen but his adult features are emerging. I can also tell you that he has the same features as you."

"What is his name?"

"Joseph Masters. Masters was Rose's last name before she moved to Calgary. Riso was her maiden name. She changed back to Masters when she left Calgary after your reported death. You did know she had a short marriage before she met you?"

There was no response.

"Michael, Rose would like to speak to you. Would you consider it?"

"She would need to come to me. I find it too difficult to travel."

"I understand. Leave it to me, but before I go, Ms Birch, you're involvement is a real question for me. Would you share it with me? It's not part of my work, but it is something that I can't get my head around."

"Dr. Fresher, let's fulfill Rose's request, then we can talk about it."

The next few hours were a blur for Fresher. He sped back to Fredericton with just enough time to drop the car off and run to catch his flight. Having missed dinner, he ate two packages of peanuts on the plane hoping it would tide him over until he landed in Toronto. The drive home to Hamilton was in the rain and the dark. By the time he got in his front door, it was well after one in the morning and he was too tired to eat. He was sound asleep after a short warm shower.

****

The next morning, he woke up famished and made an immediate to stop at a nearby restaurant. Breakfast never tasted so good. Over his second cup of coffee, he developed a plan that included speaking with Masters and giving her the news, then arranging for her visit to Bouleau. Once that was complete, the case would finally be finished.

Shortly after nine, he called Masters.

"Mrs. Masters, its Harold Fresher."

"Harold. I was waiting for your call."

"Well, I told Joey about his son and he wants to see you. There are two things you need to know; first, his real name is Michael. He can explain the name change. The second is that he has multiple sclerosis and uses a wheelchair so you will need to go to him. He is in an Eastern Canadian province; you will have to fly."

Fresher could hear Masters breathing more heavily.

"Michael?"

"Yes, and as I said, he can explain that to you. Do you want me to arrange for your visit?"

Without hesitating, she replied, "Yes."

Masters told Fresher she would be available as soon as possible.

A few minutes after she hung up, Fresher called Bouleau and his sister answered the phone.

"Ms. Birch, Rose would like to visit Michael. Are you in charge of his appointments?"

"Yes, how about tomorrow?

"All right Ms Birch, I'll make arrangements for her flight and rental."

"Dr. Fresher, before you go, Michael has a special request. He wants you here as well."

"Why?"

"We discussed this and feel that you need to hear the entire story."

Fresher hung up and shook his head. No, he thought, more secrets?

Chapter 12

Masters and Fresher flew out the following morning. As soon as the plane was in the air, Masters put her hand on his arm.

"Harold, I owe you so much. First, getting the truth about Bruno's money, and now finding Joey, I mean Michael. I never realized that he could mean so much to me after all these years."

"Mrs. Masters…."

She cut him off. "I think it's about time you called me Rose."

They arrived in Fredericton just before noon and picked up a rental car. The same clerk was on duty and did a double take when she saw Fresher. She handed him the keys as well as an application for a frequent renter membership card. Fresher left the application on the counter and walked away quickly with Masters in tow.

During the drive to the ranch, Fresher described the business and the success. Fresher could see Masters' face had a permanent smile and she laughed softly as she saw the horses in the fields. She uttered, "I hope I can ride again," a statement for herself rather than Fresher.

As they approached the gate, Fresher could see that Masters getting anxious.

"I hope Joey, I mean Michael will let me go for a horseback ride," this time the statement for Fresher. "I haven't been on one since Calgary and I always missed it."

Once through the gate and seeing the ranch house in the distance, Michael Bouleau was standing on the porch supported by forearm crutches. As Fresher pulled the car to a stop, he could see Corri Birch standing inside, looking out a window. He purposely stayed in the car letting Masters get out first. Masters opened the door, stood on the driveway and stared at Michael Bouleau.

"Hello Joey, oh I'm sorry, Michael." A few tears had welled up in her eyes.

"Hello Rosie. Its Michael Bouleau. It's been a long time."

Fresher could see Bouleau looking at Masters with a look much deeper than a casual friendship look. Masters must have seen it as well. She stepped up onto the porch, moved towards Bouleau and gave him a long hug.

"Please come inside. My sister has prepared a few things. After all, it is lunch hour."

Without any pause, Masters took Bouleau's right arm in both her hands and helped him slowly navigate to the dining table laid out with salads and sandwiches. Bouleau's sister was standing waiting for her brother and his two guests.

"Rosie, this is my sister Corri Birch. You may remember her."

Masters eyes widened and mouth opened slightly.

"Your sister? You were the person working in the convenience store. What am I missing here?"

Bouleau said, let's all sit down and enjoy a bite to eat. We have lots of time to talk.

As soon as the four sat, Masters looked at Michael and asked why the charade but Birch replied.

"I think it's best if Michael and I start at the beginning."

Fresher felt somewhat relieved that he might finally get all the answers. He also noticed that Michael and Masters were exchanging smiles.

Bouleau jumped in. "Before we start I was wondering, Rosie did you bring any photos of Joseph."

Masters quickly retrieved a small album from her purse and passed it to Michael. As he flipped through the pictures, there was no question that there was a father's pride in his face. While he was looking through the pictures, Masters was giving him a monologue of Joseph's early years and his time at school.

"Rosie, he looks like a fine young man. You have done a wonderful job. I wish now that I hadn't crumbled that paper. I'm sorry."

Masters reached over and tapped Michael's hand. It's not too late to be involved in his life Michael. It's up to you."

Fresher was anxious to hear the whole story and waited until a lull in the conversation before prompting Birch to begin.

The next several minutes were not what Fresher or Masters were expecting. In fact, it was something out of a novel.

Corinna and Michael Birch grew up in Levis Quebec. Michael was adopted by the family when he was five years old, a younger brother for seven year old Corinna that preferred to be called Corri. From the first day, he was a real hand full. Michael never finished high school moving from menial job to menial job until he earned enough money for a used car. Bored and restless, and thrown out by his adopted family, he reverted to his birth name, 'Bouleau' and eventually wound up living a nomad life on a motorcycle. Corri went in a completely different direction. She went off to college to study policing and was recruited by the Montreal Police. Within a couple of years, she went on to the RCMP working as an evidence expert. The RCMP were fighting the drug war, especially cross border trafficking but getting good information was very difficult. When their mother, Mrs. Birch passed away, Michael came back for the funeral. Michael confided in Corri that he needed to find something more meaningful than how he was living. The life he had envisioned was not as good as expected. Existing hand to mouth, taking any short-term work he could get, living in the worse places and sometimes needing to steal food to eat became the norm. He was tired of not belonging. He had no future.

Recruiting Michael to go undercover was not difficult. After some intense training and taking the alias Joey Parsons, he was ready to make his way into Dark Destiny and eventually the leader of the Skeletons. The only place where his real name and alias were connected was in highly secured files. Corri was set up as his contact and assigned to the convenience store. They worked together for a few years gathering valuable information always working towards a major bust. The rumour of an informer surfaced and Dark Destiny decided to take things into their own hands.

"That explains your involvement Ms Birch', Fresher said.

"Not entirely."

Fresher looked puzzled as Michael took over telling the story explaining that it was his job, as the trusted leader of the Skeletons, to set up the time and location of the transactions with the buyers. The opportunity of a big bust came and Michael scheduled the meeting between Dark Destiny and the buyers. Of course, Michael also informed Corri who, in turn, made sure that the ambush by the task force was set up.

"So you were arrested, tried, convicted and falsely died allowing you to get away," Masters asked.

"That's pretty well it except for the MS and the money"

Masters looked at Michael and asked, "Did you send the money to me?"

"No, Corri did."

"Corri?"

Michael confided that he told the buyers to bring two bags, $160,000 each as there would be 120 pounds of cocaine. In fact, there was only sixty pounds valued at $160,000.

Ms Birch picked up from there. "I said there was more. As soon as the area of the ambush was clear, my job was to move in to confiscate everything; bikes, cars, bodies, drugs and money. No one except Michael

113

and I knew that there was a second bag. I sent $50,000 to Rose and kept $110,000 for Michael's new life. I retired early four years ago and joined him here full time. Everything was going well until you told us about Thomas."

"Let me get this right. Dark Destiny was selling sixty pounds of drugs yet the buyers understood they were paying for twice that amount?" Fresher asked. "Surely someone had to know."

"Not necessarily," Birch responded. "To the gang, they lost the drugs and to the buyers, they lost cash. They didn't talk to each other after as both accused each other of having an informant, and the records were kept confidential. Dr. Fresher, you need to understand that we knew that Michael was in for some challenges in life. I guess you could call it a retirement bonus for Michael. Frankly, in those days there were so many busts with drugs and money floating all over the place, that kind of money would never be missed."

Michael wrapped up the discussion very succinctly. "That's the whole story."

Masters' face was frozen in blankness still absorbing what she had just heard; Fresher sat with his right hand under his chin, obviously in deep thought; Michael was staring at Masters until Birch spoke.

"You both realize that we are risking a lot by telling you this. The mob was involved so we need your word that this discussion will go no further."

Michael said, "There is still the question of how Thomas found Rose."

Fresher explained that Thomas was sent to a prison in British Columbia and Jill kept in touch. In Toronto, just by happenchance, Jill saw Rose in a bus line to Hamilton with the name 'Masters' on her suitcase tag. Sometime after that, she tells Thomas and once Thomas is released, he easily finds Rose.

"So that mystery is solved. Thanks," Michael said.

The remainder of the day, Michael and Rose spent telling each other about the past sixteen years while Birch toured Fresher around the farm. When they were leaving the larger of the two barns, Birch stopped and turned to Fresher.

"Dr. Fresher, I was in policing for a number of years and I hate to say this but I don't believe you when you told us how you got here. It took more than, 'the process of elimination'. I know Michael's files were locked. Even the Prosecutor's office wouldn't know."

Fresher tried to deny her accusation but she persisted.

"Look Dr. Fresher, we have been very honest with you."

Fresher stood by a horse stall for a few seconds before responding. "Yes Ms Birch, I did receive certain information but that is confidential and just as you expect me to keep what you and Michael told me, so I must also respect my sources."

****

Masters and Fresher left for the airport early in the evening. He never saw Masters as happy since he first met her.

"Harold, I will never be able to thank you enough. I promised Michael to come back in two weeks so we could plan for him to meet Joseph."

"Is that all you plan to do?"

"Was it that obvious, you know, between Michael and me?"

"Yes, it was."

"I know he has MS and some limitations, but just seeing him brought back those feelings I had all those years ago. I know he feels the same."

"Rose, there should be quite a bit of your retainer left. I'll make sure we get the money to you with a week."

"No Harold. You owe me nothing."

Chapter 13

With the Masters case finally closed, he looked forward to his next case being a lot simpler and he got his wish. Friday afternoon he met with new clients that hired him to track down their eighteen year old daughter that was working on a vineyard in California but apparently took off on a trip to Reno to live with a middle age man she met while he was in Napa buying wine. The parents were not happy and needed to inform her that if she didn't come back to Canada immediately, they would cut her out of any inheritance. The father gave Fresher an address in Reno where the daughter had told the vintner to forward her mail. These were the cases Fresher loved - rich clients, international travel, and no danger.

The clients left at five o'clock and he asked Samid to arrange for a Monday afternoon flight to Reno. The rest of the weekend was his to enjoy and tonight it was having dinner at Jenn's.

The week ended much better than he expected. Happy, relieved and somewhat exhausted, Fresher decided it was time for a celebration so on the way to Jenn's, he picked up a bottle of Pouilly-Fusse, her favourite white wine. As soon as he got off the elevator on Jenn's floor, he detected a faint aroma of Mexican spices. Jenn opened the door after one knock and welcomed him with a warm embrace and an extended kiss. The weekend just got a lot better.

"Something smells wonderful."

"Fish Tacos and I bought halibut."

"Perfect."

Jenn had set the table placing two red candles in the middle. He could tell that she put a lot of time into preparing for the evening.

The conversation was light with some work related anecdotes thrown in. Fresher couldn't remember that last time he laughed so much, or enjoyed the company of a woman. The kiss when he arrived was still felt and he was looking forward to many more.

After dinner, Fresher told Jenn he was off to Reno on a case on Monday but would be back by next weekend.

"Jenn, how would you like to go horseback riding when the weather gets better?"

"Horseback riding? Harold, I had no idea you rode horses."

"I haven't for quite a few years but my recent case involved a ranch and I thought it would be a change of pace."

"I have never ridden a real horse, only the ones on the merry-go-round."

"Good. It will be something special Jenn. By the way, are you still spending the day with your sister tomorrow?"

Jenn explained that she and her sister were going to Barrie to spend the day with their parents and stay over.

Just before midnight, Fresher went to the door to leave.

"I guess you won't be at Church Sunday given your business in California Monday."

"No, I have to prepare for the trip and take care of a few details on the case I just wrapped up. Next weekend?"

"Definitely, but can we delay the ranch for a few weeks?"

The goodnight embrace and kiss was longer than when he arrived. She didn't release him right away; rather, she opened her eyes and smiled.

"Don't get to much sun Harold."

As he drove home, he was contemplating how he would tell Jenn that he wanted more, much more, in their relationship. His thoughts were interrupted as soon as he opened his front door with the darkness was interrupted by the flashing red light of his telephone answering machine. He sat down, and pushed the 'Retrieve' button.

"Hello, Harold. It's Stewart Hoskins. I thought I would call and find out if you found your missing person. Hope all is well. Talk to you soon."

Odd he thought. He checked the message registry and the call was received at 10:00 p.m. that evening. Probably just a polite follow-up. He deleted the message and headed to bed thinking of Jenn Gallager.

Saturday morning Fresher awoke and his first thought was of Jenn. After showering and having a coffee, he called a local florist and arranged for a dozen roses to be sent to her Monday morning. He felt great knowing they would be a constant reminder of him while he was in Reno.

The rest of the day, he spent going to the car dealer and ordering a new car then preparing and packing for Reno. The car would be a surprise for Jenn when he picked her up late next week.

****

On his flight to Reno, after his head cleared of dinner at Jenn's, his new car and the girl's case, Corri Birch's reference to the Prosecutor's office came back to him. It was also interesting that Hoskins called him asking if he found Michael Bouleau. Fresher had been in the business long enough to know that coincidence was not always coincidence. It was something he parked in his brain for more follow-up when he was back in Canada.

It was early evening when he stepped off the plane to stifling heat. A million coloured lights from the hotels on the strip lit up the entire area turning night to day.

The hotel was a short taxi ride away and after checking in, he sampled one of the advertised buffets. On his way back to his room, he stopped in the tuck shop and bought a post card with a bright sunny beach on it. Perfect, he thought. He would mail it to Jenn later.

The following morning, Fresher retrieved the girl's address from his briefcase and stood sweating in the full sun hailing a taxi. The air-conditioned cab was a short respite until he emerged in front of adobe style classic dessert house complete with a clay tile roof and succulents planted in front. After three raps using a lion heads knocker, an older woman with an apron on opened the door.

"Si?"

"Do you speak english?"

"Yes." "

120

"Is the lady of the house?"

"One moment please."

Within a few minutes, Fresher was inside talking with the girl he was sent to find. The assignment was much easier than he expected. After delivering a short, firm message from her parents, she agreed to go back to Canada with Fresher. It wasn't until they were on the airplane that afternoon when the girl confessed she was bored with her older lover and Fresher's arrival was perfect timing. Wonderful Fresher thought, finally a case with no twists and turns.

Fresher drove back to Hamilton and dropped the girl off at her parents then drove away thinking that this was the quickest and easiest money he ever made.

As soon as he opened his door, the light from his phone flashed red in the dark room. After dropping his bag and getting a glass of water, he sat by the phone and pressed 'Retrieve' on his answering machine. The first call was from Jenn thanking him for the flowers and asking to call as soon as he got home. The second call was from Samid reminding him that he had a dentist's appointment in the morning and would be a bit late. The third call caused Fresher to sit up and press replay.

'Hello, Harold. It's Stewart Hoskins. I thought I would call and find out if you found your missing person. Hope all is well. Talk to you soon."

It was the exact same message. He thought at first that he didn't erase the first message so he pressed 'Review'. It was a second message and it came in earlier that day.

The next morning, he put the finishing touches on the Masters report as well as the report on the girl in Reno and called Hoskins.

"Stewart. It's Harold."

"Harold, thank you for calling."

"I received your messages. My apologies for not getting back to you sooner. I was in the States on a case."

"I understand. Listen I was curious if you made any headway on finding your missing person?"

Fresher detected some anxiety on Hoskins' voice and was careful knowing the confidentiality of the discussions in New Brunswick. "Yes, I did."

"That's wonderful. Where is he?"

Fresher's heart skipped a beat. He was being pressured to tell Hoskins where Bouleau was and he had no reason to know this.

"Stewart, you know that I can't tell you. That information is part of a case and I am bound to confidentiality."

"Harold, I went through a lot to get you that name. The least you can do is tell me where he is to satisfy my curiosity."

"Stewart, I do appreciate what you did. Give me a couple of days to think this over.' With that, Fresher said, 'Goodbye' and hung up.

Fresher immediately picked up the phone and called Corri Birch.

Chapter 14

"Ms Birch, you figured out that I had confidential information that helped me find ....."

She cut him off. "I thought so. You got Michael's name from the Attorney General's office that somehow accessed locked files on informants."

Fresher was caught off guard. "Let's just suppose that you are ...."

Again, she cut him off. "Look Harold, my brother's life is what you are playing with. I was in the system for twenty years and I know when there has been a leak, a purposeful leak."

Birch went on to tell Fresher that she was aware of seven undercover operatives that were assisted in finding anonymous lives after their work and three were subsequently found in the morgue within a few years. She had access to reports and knew that these people were set up. When it was Michael's turn to disappear, she made sure that his real name was buried deep in the files.

"Did you suspect anyone," Fresher asked.

"Yes."

"Let me guess, someone in the Prosecutor's office."

After a moments silence, Birch said, "Dr. Fresher, how would you like to meet me."

"When and where?"

"I will be in your office tomorrow by noon. We cannot risk you being followed here."

****

Corri Birch arrived at eleven thirty just as Samid made fresh coffee leaving the pot in Fresher's office. She had a serious look on her face and after shaking Fresher's hand, she took her coat off and sat down.

"How was your flight?"

"Good."

"Can I pour you a coffee?"

"Yes, that would be nice." After her first sip, she remarked that it was the best coffee she had ever tasted.

"Dr. Fresher, you are the one that brought the Prosecutor's office into this. Can we put all our cards on the table?"

"It's time," Fresher said somewhat relieved.

"There was a man that I suspected but could never do anything about it. He was too smart."

"Stewart Hoskins," Fresher offered.

"I thought so. How did you ever meet him?"

Fresher went on to tell Birch about meeting him in first year university, his accident, the transfer to University of Manitoba, and the chance connection through a lawyer he met on a recent case. He told her of Hoskins' seemingly initial reluctance to get information, but after mentioning the name 'Joey Parsons', he did get it for him. He related the two voice mails and recent discussion. When he thought about Hoskin's continued interest, he became very suspicious.

"So you think Hoskins is setting up operatives that you labeled as 'disappeared'?"

"Yes."

They both sat sipping coffee for a few minutes not speaking.

"Dr. Fresher, I need you to do something for me."

Birch picked up Fresher's phone. He heard a voice say hello. Birch's comments were short. "It's on. Tomorrow."

When she hung the phone up, Birch asked Fresher to call Hoskins and tell him that him that Michael Bouleau is in Gimli Manitoba living at an old motel converted to apartments on Highway 231 about a mile west of town and that he is a long haul trucker home only on Fridays.

"Ms Birch, why do I get the impression you came here with a plan?"

"Very true. I already spoke to the Director and he likes my plan and asked me to accept temporary reinstatement and be part of the team. Harold, we need to work very quickly. As I mentioned, over the years, we lost three operatives that were in new lives. This is no accident, especially the reports that they were shot. This wasn't something that the agency let known as it said that we couldn't protect our people. Everyone knew that there was an informant in the ranks, but no one could find out who. If you make the call to Hoskins, we might be able to prove Hoskins is the leak."

"Count me in on one condition."

"What would that be? You want to be paid?"

"No nothing like that. Let's wrap this up first."

"Look Dr. Fresher, at this point, you can have anything."

While Birch was sipping her second coffee, Birch coached Fresher on how to play into Hoskins' hand.

Fresher called Hoskins at his office.

"Hello Stewart its Harold."

"Hi Harold. What can I do for you?"

"I have that information you were looking for. Can you call me tonight?"

"No, you can tell me now. What changed your mind Harold?"

"You were right. There needs to be trust between old friends. Beside Stewart, I never know what cases I get next and it's great to have friends in high places."

Fresher related the exact information that Birch told him to tell Hoskins. The two men exchanged a few more pleasantries and said goodbye.

"Thank you Dr. Fresher." Birch left Fresher's office quickly, no doubt putting her plan in place.

Late afternoon, Samid walked into Fresher's office.

"Harold, I've got all the banking and accounting done and have updated your appointment book. I'm going to leave if it's okay with you."

"No problem. I was heading out early too. My new car is ready for pickup.

"A surprise for Miss Gallagher?" Samid said as he left the office.

Fresher ignored the comment and smiled to himself.

****

Friday morning, Fresher enjoyed taking his new car to the office. He took a long route and by the time he opened the door, Samid had the coffee on.

"Samid, can I see the calendar for the next month? I want to take a few days off."

"Going for a long ride in your new car?"

"You noticed?"

"Yes and it looks super."

"Thanks."

"Harold, a reminder that Mrs. Rutledge has an appointment in a few minutes."

"Did she give you any idea what she wants?"

"No, but if it is the same Rutledge that was in the paper last month, her husband was one of the top one hundred net worth individuals in Canada last year."

"Was?"

"Yes. According to the newspaper, he died of a heart attack."

At nine thirty, Samid led Mrs. Rutledge into Fresher's office. She was a much older woman, at least seventy five Fresher thought. It was obvious that she enjoyed a privileged lifestyle given her wardrobe and jewelry.

"Mrs. Rutledge, let me offer my condolences on your husband's passing."

"Thank you Dr. Fresher."

Over the next forty minutes, Rutledge described her concerns regarding her husband's death and several questions she had. Fresher took a few notes and when she appeared to be finished, he asked her what she wanted him to do.

"Simple Dr. Fresher. Where did ten million dollars go in the last year of his life? I need someone like you to tell me what happened."

"I will need a retainer. How does....."

Rutledge politely cut him off. "Here is a cheque for ten thousand dollars. Let me know if you need more."

Fresher looked wide-eyed at the cheque and almost tripped over his words. "That will be just fine. Let me do a bit of research and I'll contact you next week."

Mrs. Rutledge left Fresher's office within fifteen minutes of arriving and Fresher followed her to the door. Once it was closed he turned and handed the cheque to Samid.

"Wow Harold. This has been a banner month."

It was mid afternoon and Fresher was reading old business magazines looking for anything with the name Rutledge attached to it. Gary Rutledge had his fingers in every industry in every country. Fresher surmised that he could have spent ten million in less than a day.

The ringing of the phone tore him away from his research.

"Dr. Fresher."

"Harold, its Corri Birch. I have some news for you, excellent news."

Birch took her time telling Fresher that Hoskins' phone was being monitored and as soon as Hoskins hung up, he called a woman in Calgary and related the Gimli information stressing, 'It's Parsons.' Early that morning, three men arrived at the motel with automatic weapons. Of course, the motel was empty and the men were arrested on weapons charges."

"I didn't think that Dark Destiny was still operating."

"They weren't DD; they were mafia."

"Mafia?"

"Yes. We arrested Hoskins just after he made the call yesterday and executed a search warrant of both his office and his home. The only thing in his office of any concern was a rolodex. His house, however, was a real treasure chest. We found files on several undercover operatives including the three that were killed, each by the mafia. The file on my brother had both the names Michael Bouleau and Joey Parsons. My best guess is that they couldn't find him because Parsons was reported dead and Bouleau was virtually invisible. We also found a key to a safety deposit box that was taped inside a ledger showing several large amounts being given to him. My guess is that the box is full of cash. It wasn't until you tripped over Hoskins that he saw an opportunity to let you do the work to find Michael so he could add to his wealth."

"Is there any concern that Hoskins will implicate me in this?"

"No."

"How can you be so sure?"

"Hoskins is isolation now and we think he will cut a deal; jail time in protective custody in exchange for information on the people he worked for. Frankly, he would be a wanted man, wanted by the mob. He knows that if he implicated you that he would be jeopardizing his protection."

"Ms Birch, thank you for reporting back to me."

"You are very welcome Dr. Fresher. I should tell you that you will be receiving a cheque in the mail. It's a standard reward for our tip line. It's just enough for a good dinner – for one. By the way, you mentioned you wanted something else."

Fresher spent a few more minutes on the phone before hanging up and sitting back wondering how a seemingly simple assault turned into a case more complicated than anything he would ever have expected.

****

"Harold, a new car!"

"Yes. It was time," he said beaming. "Does steak sound good tonight?"

"Perfect."

Over dinner, Jenn could sense relief in Fresher asking if he was caught up with his case load.

"Yes, finally.

"Wonderful."

They enjoyed a prolonged dinner both ordering dessert and over coffee, Fresher reached and took Gallager's hand.

"Jenn, can you get three days off in the next month?"

"I'm sure I can. Why."

"I would like to treat you to a couple of days on a horse ranch when the weather improves."

"Now I know why you asked about horseback riding. Where?"

"A small town in New Brunswick called Woodstock."

"How did this come about?"

"If I told you how, I would be at risk of being labeled an informer."

43678332R00076

Made in the USA
Middletown, DE
27 April 2019